Teacher Abuse

Nyla Ramm

Composed in Adobe Caslon Pro and edited by GANYMEDE.

Cover by Inkysea. https://www.deviantart.com/inkysea/gallery/

Disclaimer:
All events and persons in this book depict either actual experiences of the author or disguised experiences witnessed and/or heard by her. Disguised names bear no resemblance to actual individual's names to protect their privacy. The writing is furthermore opinion with factual material shown in quotation marks as spoken or written in authoritative sources.

ISBN: 9781717928467

EMAIL: teacherabuse.nr@gmail.com

About the Author:

Nyla is a real person who directly experienced the joy of teaching and the abuses she has written about in this comprehensive documentation of "Teacher Abuse." Her preparation to teach began with a BA in History from the University of California, Berkeley, followed by a year at the U.C. Berkeley Graduate School of Education. Nyla's California Credential permitted her to teach all subjects in grades K through 8. Further testing qualified her to teach Social Studies at the high school level. As a newly minted teacher, Nyla taught 3rd grade in southern California. When newly married, Nyla and her husband moved to rural Texas where her husband had both family and military obligations and where Nyla taught. Geographically following her husband's employment changes, Nyla also experienced teaching in rural Arizona. Nyla's longest stint was in inner-city Los Angeles. With three very different states and a career lasting 30 years, Nyla experienced everything from bomb shelters to lock-downs, from kids 'carrying' to teaching gifted children, both caring and rotten administrators, and the full spectrum of experiences described in the following pages. She is passionate about the importance of public education and hopes you will feel some of her enthusiasm and passion when you finish reading.

About Facts and Figures:
This book is not meant to be a tome full of tables, percentages, and references to surveys. Where numbers or percentages are quoted, they are nominal figures, usually gleaned from common internet or news sources. It is the subjective material behind the numbers that is more important.

"Teacher Abuse" is an account of actual experiences of a long teaching career that spanned a rapid change in national and local demographics. During the same period, there was a profound change in social attitudes and behavior. The book attempts to capture the effects these changes have had on the teaching profession. Teachers were caught between tight legislative fiscal and social control and demographics. What was once an honored profession has become a scape-goat for societal changes over which they have no control. The plight of teachers described herein provides a picture of the value society places on money and a scary look at a possible future for our country.

Introduction

The public school system is a fundamental institution of the United States of America. Teachers are the backbone of that system as they interface with our children. During the recent period of societal change, teachers have come under fire for perceived and real shortcomings in public education.

The Public School System in the United States of America is the very foundation of American society. Our schools reflect our culture and change is necessary as our culture changes. The education of our children through our public school system preserves our American way of life and its institutions. Our public schools have the responsibility to prepare a literate citizenry that understands our country's history, government, culture and world position, as well as preparing our children for meaningful and productive lives. Public schools are also the primary socializing body for our children, working to develop healthy, happy and able citizens who will continue to improve and develop the society in which we live.

The buildings and grounds that house our schools are often the largest and best built buildings in a community. Even in large cities, they stand out as special and recognizable to all. These buildings serve not only as classrooms, but as public meeting places, for both educational and social events. In many of our smaller towns and cities, school sporting events are the most attended and followed activities in the community. Most of us have fond memories of our school years and remember activities such as carnivals, Halloween parades, open houses, school dances, holiday and end-of-year parties that took place on the grounds and in the rooms of our neighborhood schools. The joys of childhood, the agonies of adolescence, the satisfactions that come from promotions and graduations. These experiences connect our homes and families to our school lives and become our shared history. A large percentage of us met our spouses or partners at school. School friendships, some going back as far as kindergarten, can last a lifetime. In addition to academics, lifetime skills in sports and the arts are learned in our public schools. Professional athletes get their start in our schools, as do musicians, artists, dancers, actors and other entertainers. Learning these skills, or just being exposed to them, enriches our lives and gives us a sense of appreciation for the arts and sports.

Schools are often thought of as a child's second home, but due to major societal changes that have taken place in the United States over the last few decades, school has become the only 'home' for significant numbers of America's children. Public schools are changing, reflecting society's changes. For most of us, our home remains a stable and nurturing environment within the larger context, but for a growing percentage of our families, home as we knew it in the past, no longer exists. A major effect of societal changes has been the creation of a much larger lower class and a shrinking middle class. At the same time, the upper class has become very small and unattainable by most Americans. Our schools have been struggling to keep up with these changes and their effects on our communities, the biggest change being homelessness and poverty. Home for some is a sidewalk, shelter, car or substandard housing. Children living in these circumstances often have little food, clothing or other necessities. These children, by law, are required to attend school. Schools have become the place where increasing numbers of children receive supplemental food and even clothing. Schools are often required to remain open for longer hours to care for children during their parents working hours. The changes in our society and the consequential increased demands on our schools have been difficult to accept by those who believe the schools are changing the society, rather than a changed society forcing a change in schools.

Our public schools have become the most stabilizing element in the lives of many children, whether in small rural settings or neighborhoods within large metropolitan areas. For many of our children, school is the only stable place a child knows. For these children, their breakfast, lunch, some basic health care, and a safe environment is provided only by the school. Our schools are for everyone, not just for those who can afford to attend, but also for those who can't.

Our public schools are the life blood or our society, a tradition that we all share. Good schools are the top priority for house hunters looking for new homes and for businesses looking for new locations to either expand or start a new business. A community's schools define the community, and can make or break its future.

The public schools in the United States have a long and proud history, from rural one room school houses to world-renowned public universities. Our public schools are secular institutions, as no religious belief system is taught in our public schools, both by tradition and Constitutional Law. This is because our government is secular. The United States Constitution states:

> **Amendment I**
> "Congress shall make no law respecting the establishment of religion, or prohibiting the free exercise thereof; or abridging the freedom of speech, or of the press; or the right of the people peaceably to assemble, and to petition the Government for a redress of grievances."

Students of all religious beliefs, as well as those without religious beliefs, are welcomed in our public schools. For the greater part of our country's history Christianity has been the dominant faith of our population, especially in the more rural areas. Christian holidays have been recognized in our public schools, as well as by our business communities and government. Christian values have always been a part of the fabric of the public-school curriculum. However, teaching or practicing Christianity, or any other religion, is not a part of public-school curriculum. Prayer and Bible readings, once a normal activity in many (especially rural) schools, is no longer permitted in most public schools.

Parents wishing a religious education for their children can send them to private religious schools. The American public should not be required to use public funds for sending children to non-public schools. Religious Schools have played a large part in our history of our nation and the fabric of the culture from preschools to well respected colleges and Universities without using taxpayer's money.

Parents who desire a more prestigious private school education for their children similarly have fine choices of private, non-religious schools, also from preschool through University. However, tax money should not be used to help any student to attend a private school.

Home schooling is also a choice parents can make if they don't want to send their children to public schools, but once again, home schooling should be at the expense of the parents, not utilizing public tax monies.

Even with all of the school choices presently available to the public, over 90% of America's children still attend our public schools.

Unfortunately, our great American public-school system is under attack. A relatively small group of America's citizens have decided America's public schools are a threat to a conceptual society that they wish to impose on all of the citizens of the United States of America. The leaders of this secretive but well-funded movement have formed political action groups to implement their goals. One of the basic goals of this groups is the destruction of America's public schools. This campaign began in the mid 1970s, but most of the public has remained unaware of what is happening or why it is happening to our public schools. More will be said about this group in Chapter III. Because teachers, are the foundation of any school system, they became the first target for destruction; after all, if the foundation of our schools crumbles, everything else crumbles.

Sadly, this campaign to destroy our public schools is working. School systems are in trouble all across the nation. Some systems have substantially collapsed, and all our schools are struggling to survive in one area or another. Teachers everywhere in the United States are suffering from fiscal and/or political policies that have been enacted by our local, state and federal governments reflecting the wishes of only that small segment of the population bent on destroying our public schools.

A large portion of America's citizenry don't care about, or even notice, what is happening to our schools, but teachers have noticed and the have decided 'enough-is-enough' and are finally speaking up. The way teachers and our schools have been treated over the past 40 years is appalling and actually to most, unimaginable.

Teachers are the base of any school system; the very foundation of our public schools. Teachers are intelligent and highly educated. Teachers are proficient in their subjects, and methods of teaching them to our children. Teachers are being blamed for the very real decline in student test scores. It is claimed, and may appear logical, that if test scores are down, then students aren't being properly taught by our teachers. While this argument may appear logical, it is completely fallacious. Yet, due to the abuse, ridicule and blame teachers have received for both the perceived and real decline of our educational system, it appears to many that unqualified teachers must be the cause of the decline in learning. If that is true, potential teachers, plus those already certified, should be required to meet still higher standards to be employed. Qualifications for teacher certification have steadily increased over the past forty years. To qualify for teacher certification, one must have a BA or BS degree, specialized teacher training, normally an extra year in a graduate program that includes student teaching, plus the requirement to pass extensive post graduate exams. Only then can they become certified teachers. A high percentage of teachers also obtain Masters Degrees, and some even PhD s. In other words, teachers are well educated and have proved they understand both their subjects and how to teach them, before they even enter a classroom.

Despite the fact that teachers have met these qualifications, teachers are no longer respected by the public. The groups that have set out to destroy our public educational system have succeeded in undermining our teachers. Teachers are rarely asked their opinion about education, yet being in the 'front lines,' they are probably the best sources of intimate knowledge in the country about children and the best means to provide for their education. Teachers learn about their students from the students themselves. Our children are a reflection of their homes and families, and thus our society. Teachers hear about students' daily activities, and what happens at home and in society. Teachers are familiar with our electronic devices, how they are used, and how their use is changing both our language and societal behavior. They are privy to the latest fads and styles. They know where their students live, with whom they live, and what their parents do for a living. Teachers know if a child has been abused, if someone in a child's family is in jail, if a child has been a victim or a recipient of violence, if parents are pushing a child too hard for the child's health and where a child goes after school. Teachers know how their student's parents feel about the teachers and how they perceive their place in society. But most of all, teachers know what our children are thinking, how they act, how they view society and see their place in it.

Teachers gain all this knowledge because they are with our children five days a week for an average of six hours a day, often more waking hours than the children spend with their parents. Our children are in the hands of our teachers from preschool through university. Yearly records of all students are maintained by teachers, as prescribed by law, and these records contain every report card, test score, special education and attendance record from kindergarten through 12th grade. Students voluntarily tell teachers what is going on in their families and teachers are required to report suspected parental abuse. Often, teachers are the only adults aware of a child's problems.

Teachers care very much about America's children, all of them, no matter what their situation. A teacher is often the only caring adult a child can count on to help them with their problems or to show them any love or care.

Teachers make up a vast reservoir of knowledge of our society, but are rarely asked to help solve, or even venture an opinion about the state of our nation or are they asked how we might be able to solve our nation's educational problems or any other of our nation's problems.

The public is much more aware now that our schools are in trouble. Teacher walk- outs and strikes in several of our states have pushed the problem of education to the fore, but we need to keep up the fight, or nothing is going to change. I have found evidence of teacher abuse in all parts of the United States and although different segments of the country seem to suffer differing forms and degrees of abuse, abuses are prevalent everywhere. Teachers are in trouble, and they need help.

There was an interesting column in my local paper the other day: The columnist began her article by saying that she was as tired as everyone else of hearing about, and reading about, the subject of education. She really empathized with teachers who, in the final analysis, aren't all bad. She even qualified her statement further by saying that there are less than perfect professionals in other endeavors as well, after which she proceeded to blast just one more teacher.

Although I am used to reading such articles as they may be seen daily. What made this one particularly irritating was the assumption the columnist made that her statements were factual. For instance, she first equated most of education's problems with teachers. Secondly, she assumed that the only problem teachers have is one of stupidity, and thirdly, with great dispassion, she called the subject of education not worth any deeper thought. Thinking about this article for quite some time, it was clear to me why this obviously intelligent, educated person would think the subject of education not worth any further thought. The columnist believed the problem in our public schools had been discovered, authenticated and isolated. Her opinion was that the faults in education lie totally with teachers. Therefore, there is really nothing else to discuss. Much of the public, and even more frighteningly, our politicians, believe this to be true. New legislation requiring teacher competency tests, tougher teacher educational requirements, merit pay proposals and other measures are being imposed in nearly every state in the Union. Teachers have been tried and convicted for the poor quality of education which presumably exists in our country today. News Media reports have concentrated on their perception of the poor quality of our nation's teachers. Frequent comments go something like this: "How can a student be taught by a teacher who himself is too dumb to learn the subject" or "Teachers come from the bottom of their graduating class," or to rephrase an old cliche, "If they can't do it, they teach it."

Because of the weakened position of teachers in society, they have become a political football and a scapegoat for politicians. Teachers, for reasons discussed in more depth in another chapter, have little ability to fight off their attackers and, therefore continue to be attacked. Politicians, through the use of the media, insist that statistics prove that our children aren't learning at an acceptable level in our public schools. Our students' test scores are constantly being compared to student test scores in other advanced nations and we are always at or near the bottom. Prospective employers complain about the poor abilities and incompetence of high school graduates. Statistics do show that test results are poorer. These statistics are then used to imply that our nation's teachers are at fault.

The statistics constantly quoted do not mean less teaching is going on in the classroom. Even if there is less student achievement, it does not necessarily equate that teachers are not doing their job or are the source of the problem. Public opinion polls show that the nation perceives the country as having a very poor overall public education system.

Our children have every opportunity to receive an excellent education and our teachers are perfectly capable of providing it. Education is in trouble, but not for the reasons many have come to accept as truth. The reputation of our teachers is shot. They have been convicted and legislatively sentenced all over the nation, not in just one or two regions. Teachers throughout the United States are being abused. They are taking a 'bum rap' for some commonly held opinions that aren't true. The politicians are misreading the problems of teachers and education; if this misreading continues, our educational woes will only escalate. The only result of present legislative cures to make teachers, and thus education, better, has been the elimination of good teachers at a record rate. Money, politics, and social change are behind teacher abuse, not the inabilities of teachers. But, if the public doesn't wake up to the fact that our schools are being attacked, public schools will collapse, and the 90% plus of our nations' children who depend on public schools will have little or no opportunity for an education.

Teachers, just as any other professionals, do have problems, but their problems have very little to do with personal inabilities, even though that is an area where they are constantly on the defensive. One teacher abuse of which everyone seems to be aware is the low pay scale. The consensus is that the teacher difficulty can be solved by paying higher wages; that this would produce better teachers. There is no quarrel whatsoever with the fact that teachers must be better paid. Some states pay their teachers far better than others, but across the board, teachers must receive more money.

It's not just the lack of buying power due to the low pay that teachers endure either, it also involves a feeling of betrayal. Teacher salaries simply do not compensate for the amount of education a teacher must obtain, or for the actual quantity of teaching time, preparation and administrative work now required. Low salaries also demonstrate the low opinion the public as well as politicians hold for teachers. Teachers both need and deserve higher compensation.

Poor pay is a major problem for teachers and one of the worst ways in which they are being abused. But their problems go far deeper and are more complex that just low wages. Poor teacher performance, which, more realistically is poor student performance being interpreted as poor teacher performance, is another major cause of teacher abuse.

Teachers are being attacked for something that isn't their fault. Our teachers do not lack ability, nor are they stupid. Teachers are not getting through to many of their students for a multitude of reasons, most of which deal with the fact that our children are coming to school unprepared or unable to learn. Teachers cannot learn for their students. In the next chapter, reasons why students can't learn will be discussed.

There are still adequate supplies of good teachers. Teacher requirements in each state are just as tough or tougher than they were twenty years ago. For reasons that will become clearer in the following pages, many well qualified and available personnel are no longer in the classrooms. The tens of thousands of good and competent teachers who are in the classroom are saddled with a multitude of reasons why they aren't perceived as succeeding in their field – most have nothing to do with inability to teach or even the low pay.

Due to the problems and abuses, teachers are leaving the field in droves. Morale of the nation's teachers is at an all-time low. What are some of the other reasons for their disenchantment? The hundreds of teachers interviewed, both employed and unemployed in their chosen field, have had a lot to say about the abuses in the profession – low pay was rarely the only reason given for their disillusionment. The problems facing our nation's teachers are complex; pay raises alone are not going to solve the grievances which plague these professionals or alone fix our educational system's problems. The public, politicians and even school administrators should take note because if action isn't taken soon to stop this teacher abuse, we as a nation, will wind up with exactly what we deserve, a teaching profession crippled beyond repair.

Abuses

Changes in society's mobility plus increasingly centralized control of the public school system have made life miserable for teachers. Concentration on cost and 'efficiency' have decreased teachers' social standing in the eyes of the public. 'The Right' aims to destroy public education.

During the past 50 years public school teachers have gradually lost most of the elements that made teaching a rewarding and respected occupation. The decline in pay has been devastating, and likely the most significant loss because today's society equates income with success. But low pay isn't the only abuse in the ever-growing quantity of abuses teachers endure. The stories in this chapter were related to me by other teachers, and it contains my own story as well. They relate actual happenings from the early 80's to the present. These stories illustrate the many indignities teachers endure each and every day.

Robert

Robert went into teaching because he wanted to coach. His life's ambition was to become a head football coach at the high school level. He planned to coach for several years and then go into administration. Therefore, his college curriculum was academic with a minor in physical education. His grades were good and his score on the National Teacher's Examination, an excellent 1300. After graduation his coaching dream came true. In the first year after college he was hired as a head Junior Varsity football coach and science teacher. Robert was single and prepared for the low pay. He loved football and coaching so much he might have coached without pay. Robert taught and coached for two years before leaving the field for an executive position at triple the pay. The low salary was not the reason Robert left teaching; it was disillusionment with the system.

Robert quickly learned that the pecking order at his school placed the teachers at the very bottom. If a parent questioned a grade or even a coaching decision, no matter what the level of the parent's educational background or ability or lack of knowledge about a particular situation, the parent was always correct. The principal, who would be expected to back his teachers, was quick to take the side of the parent. Parents and students were also encouraged to evaluate the teachers on a regular basis, either in written or verbal form. These evaluations were often used by the principal in his formal evaluation of the teacher. A student counselor would tell the students, in the presence of the teacher, to please report anything the teacher might do that the students didn't like or with which they felt uncomfortable. The teachers had very little disciplinary power and the students readily took advantage of this. Robert and the other teachers had to wait in the cafeteria line with the students if they wanted to purchase their lunch. Because ten minutes of their twenty-five minute lunch was duty time, they rarely had time to eat. Secretaries, janitors and cafeteria workers were uncooperative and condescending to the teachers. Robert would run up against so many obstacles just getting equipment or lines drawn on the field that he would often do these tasks himself. Robert had no say in what he was to teach the students in class because of a strictly prescribed syllabus provided by the school, and he was not allowed to flunk a student, as administrative harassment precluded the effort. Robert felt his hands were tied. The thrill and satisfaction he had so long envisioned simply was not there and he couldn't respect himself.

Robert's story is a compilation of several similar stories and is not overstated. This case points to the problems teachers face every day as they go about their duties. Teachers experience hostility from students, parents, clerical help, janitorial, cafeteria workers, and administrators. Teachers no longer have the respect of the public, school administrators and non-certified staff. Both newly certified and experienced teachers aren't considered capable of student evaluation, student discipline or even planning their own lessons. Teachers are watched by clerical and janitorial help to make sure they are doing their job, and if a teacher, in their opinion, makes a mistake, the non-certified personnel make certain the administration is told of the wrong-doing. Often these mistakes are as minor as forgetting to empty the classroom trash cans or locking a door.

Captain McDonald

Capt. McDonald was retired military. He had spent twenty years in the service but was too young to quit working. Thus, he decided to fulfill a lifetime ambition to teach, by returning to school for teacher training. It took three semesters to get his teaching certificate and begin his new career. By Christmas time of his first year he was ready to quit. It was not the students' lack of academic and behavioral discipline that caused Capt. McDonald's problems. It was not the low pay, as he had a substantial pension; it was the pressure, subtle and not so subtle, from the outside.

Because he had been a military officer for so many years, the McDonald's had learned the many social graces required to please foreign diplomats as well as local dignitaries and high ranking military. Capt. McDonald, had not a qualm about relocating for a new teaching position, but he and his family were not prepared for the complete lack of social and political respect they received at their new location. They joined a local club, open to anyone in their upper middle class neighborhood and proceeded to try to make friends. Capt. McDonald, who had been accustomed to conversing with the nation's leaders, was humiliated to find men actually turning their backs on him to talk to others. A teacher's opinion was not worth much to their new neighbors. Mrs. McDonald was afraid or ashamed to tell her new workout club members that her husband was a teacher. She would, instead, say he was retired. Their teenage children received far less respect from other students and had a much harder time adjusting to the new school environment. Capt. McDonald did not sign a contract for the next year.

As Capt. McDonald discovered, teachers all around the country, those with years of experience as well as those new to the profession, are becoming social outcasts, too inferior to be a part of society's mainstream. Car salesmen and Realtors are barely polite when they discover a potential customer is a teacher. Teachers, who are constantly being told by administrators that they are professionals, receive few of the courtesies or privileges accorded other professionals in our society. Increasingly, this highly educated group is driving old cars, unable to buy a home, go out to dinner, or even buy decent clothing. All these things add to the poor image and lack of respect already so prevalent. Teachers receive very little respect in their communities, fostered by the bad publicity in recent years.

Jennifer

Jennifer was an honor student both in high school and college. She majored in mathematics with a minor in secondary education, and graduated Magma Cum Laude. Swimming was her special love and she had coached a local club's swim team to several league championships during her summer vacations. She loved children and was a good coach. Teaching, she thought, would offer the same rewards as coaching, plus, she could continue her summer job. The salary was fairly good for a single woman her age. She wasn't at all hesitant about taking a position; in fact, she was excited about her new career. Jennifer however, taught only one year before leaving for a job in industry. During the year she taught, she saw or heard negative media reports about teachers each stating over and over again that teachers were *all* from the lower half of their graduating class and that they were inferior students, not capable of teaching their subjects. Jennifer, who had been at the top of her class, was too embarrassed to admit that she was a teacher and fled to industry where her past accomplishments and learned skills were appreciated not only monetarily, but with respect to her abilities.

Because of the abuse to which they are being subjected, many teachers, are looking for jobs in other fields and would like to leave teaching for a better paid, more rewarding and a more respectable profession, but not all are able to make the change. Jennifer was able to move into industry because of her educational background in math and computer science, and because of her age and limited teaching experience. Teachers are not the only ones who pay attention to the media. The public has formed their own opinions of teachers, and these are not good. Teachers who have taught for any length of time suffer the same lack of credibility in the job market as they do in society as a whole. Many teachers, especially those in their forties, who have felt the growing abuse of their profession, cannot escape and now feel trapped and disillusioned. But those who can are moving to other professions and the teaching field is feeling their loss. No one wants to read or hear that he/she, because of their chosen occupation, is at the bottom of society's heap. The cruelest point is, however, that just like Jennifer, teachers are not stupid, and they do not naturally come from the bottom of their graduating class. Yet the constant condemnation throughout the media is making it very hard for these highly educated, certified, credentialed, licensed, and dedicated people to hold up their heads.

My Story

One of my family's moves took us to one of the southern states. I had to qualify for that state's teachers license. It took several months to obtain the license. Since I couldn't yet apply for a teaching position, I applied for a job with what was then called Southern Bell, and went to work at a phone store taking service orders, and either selling or leasing phones. I had to take a couple of tests to qualify for my new job, but I don't remember that more than a high school diploma was required for my new position. Working in that job raised my self esteem to a whole new level. I hadn't realized how much my self esteem had been damaged by teaching school. At my new place of employment, workers were given breaks, a lunch hour, enough time to actually go out to lunch, praise for a job well done, and all in a friendly, noncompetitive atmosphere. I was in heaven, and the pay wasn't bad for a non-management position. My educational background was a plus, as I was able to learn the job quickly. I was soon reporting the day's intake and sales though a special phone system, and writing letters for my fellow workers. The chief difference between this job and teaching was that I was being thanked and shown respect for my efforts. I eventually received my teachers license for that state, and substituted a few times, but my family relocated once again, and I went back to teaching in a new state with a new attitude plus the desire to change what was happening to our nation's schools.

A teaching career can last a long time; some of today's teachers began their careers 40 years ago. The public believes what the media and other informants say about teachers to be fact, that teachers are unqualified to do their job. Teachers have no real means of rebuttal. This view of teachers has been used by the media to explain why students aren't doing well on tests and not learning what they should be learning. The primary cause of poor student performance lies not with the teachers, but with societal factors. Teachers are being abused and battered for all kinds of reasons that have little to do with actual teaching. It is very easy for parents, and others responsible for child welfare to blame teachers for all of society's failings. False accusations are hard to take and America's teachers are being abused by almost every sector of our society.

When I was teaching in a K – 6 school in the early 90's, a teacher friend who was teaching 3rd grade at the same school apparently hadn't cleaned her school room sink as well as the principal thought it should be cleaned. On the last day of school for that year, the principal came into that teacher's room before the students had been dismissed and bawled the teacher out, in front of the students, for this egregious offense, and made her scrub the sink again. This teacher had been teaching for about 20 years at the time, was known to be a good teacher, was married to a banker, had two children in high school, was active in her church, and belonged to several social and community service groups. This particular principal was not well liked and had abused several other teachers at the school, so this wasn't an isolated case of teacher abuse at this particular school. The repercussion from this particular incident was the loss of a good teacher, because my friend transferred to a better school over summer break. The principal eventually had his comeuppance. In the district where this incident took place, principals were paid according to the total number of students enrolled in that particular school, and this school had about 1200 students. I later learned that the abusing principal had been transferred to a school with about 400 students. This is the only time I recall that justice for teachers was served.

Teachers are now responsible for cleaning their rooms, and often the school yards as well, in districts throughout the United States. They are required to take on janitorial work for no extra pay, and with no extra time. Teachers are also required to be teaching the entire time that students are in the classroom, and in one district where I taught, not even allowed to sit at their desks when the children were in the room – as they must be teaching at all times. Teachers must do their lesson plans, grade student papers, keep parents informed about their students progress and behavior, teach, take care of discipline, be aware of a student's health concerns, and take care of their janitorial duties all within their prescribed work day. Much of the time they don't have time for lunch, bathroom breaks, and certainly no coffee breaks! Teachers do all this for far lower pay than most college graduates in any other field.

In financially strapped districts, everything is cut back, one of the first being maintenance and janitorial tasks. The teachers are asked to do them because teaching positions can't be cut any further. Doing these tasks degrades them and in the eyes of others. This type of teacher abuse appears to be more rampant in the low paying states, or schools in low income areas. You might think this makes sense as, surely, districts that pay less will draw less qualified teachers. This has not been found to be true. Low paying states require the same degrees and tests from teachers as the high paying states. It is because the lower paid teacher commands little or no respect.

Teachers are given very little freedom in the classroom to teach in their own way and are rarely invited to share in the planning process that dictates what is to be taught or how it is to be taught. The subject matter and the methods to be used are decided on by administrators, school boards, private consulting firms, the public, publishing companies, and even public officials. The decisions made by these groups don't necessarily improve teaching methods and are often made for political or ideological reasons, rather than to benefit students or teachers. Teachers are required to teach using the methods adopted by their districts. Teachers who have years of teaching experience and years of education in their subject areas should have a respected part in the planning process, but they don't. Teachers are often made to use teaching methods that they know will not work, but they are not part of the selection process.

In the early 2000's I taught 6th grade in a small town in Southern Arizona. The administrators in that district were the best I ever had, and during the six years that I taught there, I experienced some of the best teacher - administrative relationships in my entire career. The problems in that school of poor, mostly minority students, many from dysfunctional families, with a physical plant having below standard facilities and very few supplies was very similar to the situation I had faced in Southern California; because it was a small and close knit town, the atmosphere was completely different and I was happy to be there. It was however, an academically poorly achieving school. This caused, the state to intervene with a new first grade reading program that required every first grade teacher to teach exactly same thing, in the exact manner, at exactly the same time every day. State representatives were sent to the school to monitor the program and ensure that each of the teachers were doing precisely as they had been told. If a teacher found not to be at the exact part of the lesson at the exact time the teacher was disciplined. The result of this situation was an almost 100% turnover of first grade teachers after the first year of the program and little or no gain in test scores. Teachers know what the results would be of such a program; they are just never asked. The fact that teachers are not asked for their input as to how things should be taught is just another way the lack of respect for teachers manifests itself.

In a Southern California district where I taught in a very poor neighborhood for fifteen years, the teachers were constantly required to write new standards to make the curriculum more rigorous and attend workshops to learn new and better teaching methods using new expert-designed programs 'guaranteed' to raise test scores. None of the programs made any difference to the test scores. New programs were begun each year because the test scores remained low. Each new program should have been given at least a three year trial period, but that never happened. Change was constant, and the teachers were required to learn a new program every year, if not every semester. Learning so many new programs is hard on teachers, is very expensive, and rarely works. Lack of sufficient school funding meant that often the new materials needed to properly implement the new program were only partially provided, and there was never enough time to prepare. The teachers could have solved many of the school's problems just by changing schedules and using skills and successful methods learned from years of experience, but teachers were completely disregarded by all of those in charge. Furthermore, teachers were blamed for not executing the programs properly or sabotaging them.

Text book companies, test producing companies and educational supply companies charge high prices for their products and their purported expertise. School districts purchase text books and other school supplies from salespeople who visit individual schools to hawk their wares and put on very persuasive shows. Often, a program will be chosen that consists of more materials than just the text books, but because of financial concerns, the district will purchase only the text books, and sometimes only one set of text books for each classroom. If there is only one set of text books in a room and that room's teacher has five classes, five sets of students use one set of books. When that is the case, students can never take a book home or be able to call a book their own. When the books are used by more than one student a day, they become soiled, marked up and shabby long before replacement dates for the texts is scheduled. To teach effectively when supplemental materials were not ordered, teachers often purchase the extras themselves. Teachers spend many hours of out of school time plus their own money on such projects. Teachers need not only to be better paid, but they need to be furnished all necessary materials.

Not only is money not spent on teachers' pay and teaching materials, very little is spent on school structures. Many schools have leaky roofs, peeling paint, dirty classrooms, shabby auditorium seats and stage curtains, filthy or inoperative restrooms, broken air conditioning and heating systems, and trashy yards. Teachers might have a teachers lounge that is furnished with a battered table and six or so battered and mismatched chairs, a soda machine, and two one stall bathrooms with doors that open up right into the lounge area. Rarely does a school have a teachers' cafeteria. Good school environments are more conducive to both learning and teaching.

Teachers also feel helpless when it comes to classroom discipline. Again, there is implied inadequacy in this area, not due to their past performance, but from policy changes. At present, teachers have very little authority in disciplinary matters. In most public schools in the United States, counselors, principals, vice-principals or special teachers have the ultimate disciplinary authority. The consequence of removing that authority from teachers is that students have no trouble figuring out who is boss in the classroom and taking full, and sometimes outrageous, advantage of the situation.

Often, a student will misbehave in the classroom by being disruptive, disrespectful, or by just not doing the work. When asked by the teacher to please get back to work, he/she will not comply, the student will let the teacher know in devious ways that he/she will not behave and that he/she doesn't have to. After several attempts, the teacher will refer that student to a counselor. After a short time, the student returns, smirking, swaggering and continuing the same pattern of misbehavior. The counselor will then call the teacher for a conference about this student. The teacher will be asked to prove that the student did indeed misbehave; then, he/she is told to use a different voice with this student as the student has found the teacher's mannerisms offensive. The counselor has found no reason to take any disciplinary action for the student.

Teachers should have the ability to discipline the students, but their hands are tied by administrative policy, the law and parents. Teachers have actually been sued by parents for 'abusive' discipline. Most of the time in such cases, the parents are not awarded judgments, but just the threat of a lawsuit is enough to keep a teacher 'in his/her place'. The law favors the student, and until many attitudinal and judicial changes are made, it will be hard, if not impossible, to bring discipline back into the schools. Let's make one thing clear: discipline is not corporal punishment. Corporal punishment is not necessary to have discipline.

When I was teaching at a middle school I had a student in the 6th grade who was known for taking things that weren't his, being disruptive in class, and not doing his work. This student was in my homeroom, and three of his other teachers and I got together with the counselor to discuss what could be done to modify this behavior. We decided the parent of this student should come to school and go class to class with the child. On the agreed day the student and a man calling himself the child's father came to my homeroom class. During class time the student took one of the other student's backpack. I saw this and reported it to the counselor. A meeting was set up for right after school for the student, his father, the counselor and me. During the meeting we learned that the father was actually one of the child's stepfathers, if I recall correctly, the 3rd, and that he no longer lived with the student. The child explained to us that it is OK to take someone's property if "you really really needed it, or if you really – really wanted it." The stepfather agreed and truly thought that the boy had done nothing wrong. After they had gone, the counselor and I decided a home visit would be the next step taken in order to find a way to help this child. It turned out that the child lived with his grandmother, along with several cousins and others, in an old one room garage conversion, where a sheet was being used for a front door. The student continued to be in my class and no further action was taken. Multiple reasons are contributing to our schools disciplinary problems. Our society's failings, poor parenting, restrictive laws, and the lack of respect for teachers are major factors.

I have taken many workshops on classroom management and discipline as a teacher, but one stands out in my mind because of the absurdity of the solutions offered. One lecturer told us that we should ask the janitor to put tennis balls on the legs of one of our student desks, screw a pencil sharpener on the desk, then build a little nook in the corner of the room for the desk so that the teacher could put the one misbehaving student at that desk; then, the teachers problems would be over! Yes, that actually happened. The supposed ex-teacher must have taught in a school that still had janitors, 29 well behaved students out of a class of 30, a room of his/her own, permission to build a structure in the room, an extra desk that could be altered, and parents and administrators who would allow such isolation of a student. I don't recall a single situation like that in any of the schools in which I have taught.

One of the schools in which I taught was on a three track system due to an overpopulation of students. This is how the system worked: The student body was divided into 3 equal groups, A, B and C. Each group was on track, meaning attending school, for 4 months, and off track for 2 months, and then on track for 4 months, and off again for two months during each school year. One group was always off track while two were on track. The school year was from July 1 to June 30, thus the school was in session all year long every year. There was never a school day that the building wasn't in full use. When A track ended on June 30, the new B track teacher and students would be in an A track teacher's room the very next day. The only days that the school wasn't occupied were Christmas Day, New Years Day, Easter, plus a few national holidays. I recall that school was held one year on Christmas Eve. Because the school was located in a very undesirable area, teachers had neither weekend nor after-hours access to the school. Thus, most of their non-teaching work had to be done at home.

The abuses teachers endured in this school were the worst I have ever heard about, and the worst I have personally endured, but some of the same abuses take place at other schools. Teachers in schools using track systems never have their own room, and never have a single day in which they are alone in the room with no students present. Each time a teacher comes back on track they are in a different room from the previous session. Because the new room was occupied by another teacher and students on the previous day, there is never enough time to put up bulletin boards, decorate, or even clean, to prepare the room for a new crop of students, yet the teachers are held to the same standards for room environment as all other teachers in non-track situations. Lesson planning is usually done either during a single free period during the day or at home. This school had a difficult time finding substitute teachers, so regular teachers were often required to cover other classes during their free period, leaving no time for planning, grading, or even going to the restroom. These 'track' teachers were held to the same standards for lesson plans as all other teachers. This school had only a single set of textbooks for each academic subject taught in that room, so as many as 18 different groups of students used the same set of books during an academic year. Other supplies, such as paper, pencils, colored pencils, graph paper, tag board and markers were very scarce. There was only a single 25 minute lunch period a day for almost 1,400 students, teachers and administrators.

Teachers at this school could substitute-teach during their off-track time to make a little extra money, and since there were always classes without teachers, we were guaranteed to have a substitute position if we wanted one, and I took one of those positions quite often during the time I taught there. Substitutes were paid fairly well because there was a great need for them. When I took one of the positions, I knew I would only be working for 21days, because on the 22nd day in those positions, the pay increased and additional benefits began. If a new permanent teacher for that class had still not been found, a different substitute teacher was hired for that particular class so that the pay would revert to the lower rate. Sometimes, if a permanent teacher couldn't be found, a substitute would be hired for one day, then the previous sub would be re-hired at the lower rate. Many times, a class would have substitute teachers for the length of the time on track.

One might wonder why I stayed at that school for such a long time? The reason is because I was a fully credentialed teacher and the school was required to have a staff of at least 50% fully credentialed teachers or it would be out of compliance with state regulations. If a fully credentialed teacher was offered a transfer to a different school within the district, the principal of their current school had to give his/her permission to take the new job. I was offered a dream job teaching history at one the local high schools, but my principal would not let me go.

The student body at the time I taught there was composed of approximately 25% blacks and 75% Hispanics, mostly of Mexican decent. The school and the community had been going through a very rapid transition from an all black School to a mixed race school. Rapid cultural changes such as this produce many secondary effects, difficult for the staff to either predict or manage. Consequently, all involved, students and their families, teachers, and administrators were suffering from the very significant changes taking place in their lives. Although there was no plan to address any of the problems caused by this social change, school performance continued to be judged by the same criteria as all other schools in the state.

The school's neighborhood was gang and drug invested infested, violent, dirty and rundown. The majority of students had family members, or were themselves victims of drive by shootings. Many lived in substandard housing and had little food or clothing. Very few students lived with both genetic parents. The great majority lived with at least one step parent, with grandparents, older siblings, aunts, uncles, or others. Many of our students' parents and other relatives were in jail, and some of the students had done time in juvenile hall. Most of the students came to school unprepared to learn. Yet, once again, teachers were expected to teach using traditional techniques, using one failed method after another, with very little success.

Of course, discipline at this school was very difficult and often took up the majority of class time. One work shop on discipline was given at the school by a world famous organization that had done lots of good work with disadvantaged and hard to control children. Their proposed solution was to take a misbehaving student out into the hallway or into a corner of the room, get down to his or her level, quietly explain to them what they were doing was wrong, and suggest an alternative way to react to this particular situation. Each teacher was provided with a script to use when speaking with the student. Obviously, this group did not understand that if a teacher has a class of approximately 30 students, at least half of whom have chronic issues with bad behavior, the teacher can't walk out into the hallway, remain there for 5 or 6 minutes, and come back into the room, without complete chaos erupting in that classroom. Such a plan might work if very few children were in the room, supervised by another adult.

Another disciplinary, as well as professional tool that has been taken away from teachers is the right to give earned grades. Many school systems across the country do not permit student failure. Teachers cannot give failing grades, even when the student has done very little work. The teacher is thus left with no means of discipline, either behavioral or academic. In one Southern California middle school, the teachers were told that if a child was given an F in a class it was the teachers fault. A solution offered by administration called for the teachers to teach to all of the students by making individual lesson plans for each child, by using several different teaching methods, such as hands on, visual and auditory, and by making the lessons understandable to the level of competence of each student. Teachers typically had 150 students per day in 6 classes. If a teacher planned, as asked, for a plan for each student, taking ten minutes each to prepare, it would total 1500 minutes, or approximately 22 hours a day just to plan the lessons. Ridiculous? Not only that, but the students were never held accountable in any way, for either their studies or their behavior.

Teachers are held to absurd standards in all manner of situations every day. Teachers have become responsible, not only for their own performance, but for that of the students, parents and administrators as well. Most teachers like teaching, care very much for their students, and don't want to quit or lose their jobs. Yet just surviving in such a situation is difficult. Teachers often have to compromise their own standards just to keep functioning and sane. Most teachers in that situation would eliminate F's, and just give A-D grades.

Parents are often more responsible for grades being given to students than students themselves. Parents who have children in gifted classes, or those taking AP classes, don't understand that a gifted child doesn't automatically get A's because they are gifted. Gifted children in gifted classes are given a more rigorous version of the same curriculum as regular classes. They still have to do the required work, take the tests, and follow specified standards of behavior. The work they turn in and the tests they take are still graded on a curve. A gifted student who truly earns an "A" in a gifted, or AP class, shouldn't have to have their A work's worth diminished by also giving A's to the gifted who do sloppy work, don't turn in their work, and get lesser grades on tests. Both students and teachers understand this, but parents and administrators don't like this and often make unreasonable demands on the teachers to raise marks to better, unearned grades.

Students taking college qualifying, or placement tests, such as the SAT's are allowed to take the test multiple times plus take classes on how to take the test, until they make a high enough score to to reach collage application levels. This practice also diminishes the scores of the students who could only take the test once to achieve the needed level. It would appear, on the surface, that we have many more qualified college bound students who have very high grade point averages, high SAT scores, and who are active both in school and community activities than ever before. But in reality, many of these students didn't really earn the grades on their transcripts or the scores on their tests. Thousands of these students are applying to all of the best schools, but only a few of these students are getting their first, or second choices, nor should they, and many are even being turned down by their 'for sure' schools.

The dual practices of giving unearned grades and being able to take tests over and over, is not helping our children receive a good education. It doesn't necessarily mean they will do well in college and they aren't prepared for failure or real life disappointments. They have an unrealistic view of themselves and don't understand true responsibility. We should be letting our children reach their natural level and take as long as they need to do so. They would be much happier, have much less stress, and probably do much better in life. Teachers know this, but no one listens to us.

Dianne

Diane is forty-two years old. She is a graduate of the University of Kansas with a major in English and a minor in Early Childhood Education. She taught in Kansas for three years after her graduation at the age of twenty-two before her husband's job took them to another state. Diane had no trouble getting a teaching position near her new home, but in order to get that state's teaching certificate, she was required to take a three-unit United States History course. This was somewhat of a problem in that the nearest university where the class was taught was over fifty miles away. This state also required five additional units every five years in order to keep the certificate current. Diane lived in this state two years before her husband's job took the family to yet another state.

Diane had a very difficult time getting a job in this third state and wasn't hired until after the start of the school year, and then, only because the district was in desperate need of an extra teacher. This puzzled Diane, who had always gotten superior ratings for her teaching performance, plus all her credentials were in order. Diane was again required to take a three-unit state history course in order to receive that state's certification. By the time the her family had to move again, Diane had taught eight years, had accumulated fifteen units past her BA. and was certified to teach in three different states. She had no idea her teaching career was over.

Her problems began in the fourth state even though she had no trouble getting state certification. She did not even have to take the required history course. She was, however, unable to get a job. The fourth state required teachers attain a Masters Degree within five years after being hired, and although Diane had fifteen graduate units, she presumed that she was not hired because she was not even close to having a Masters Degree. Her recommendations were excellent and her transcript had not changed. Thus, she went back to school and in two semesters received her degree. Diane did not get a job the next year nor for the remaining five years she was in residence. She remained puzzled about her inability to get a teaching position.

Applying for and receiving a certificate in the fifth state, Diane, always the optimist, interviewed with high hopes at the several school districts in the vicinity of her new home, but her optimism was quickly squelched. The personnel director of one of the systems told her flatly that he did not like her experience or her advanced education. She was simply could not be hired as a teacher in his district because she would cost too much money. They only hired teachers with three years or less of experience and no Masters Degree. Diane was outraged. She was a good teacher and she knew her years of experience and advanced education had only added to her teaching ability. Surely there must be another reason, some failure of which she was unaware. She was so upset over the personnel director's explanation that she wrote her congressman in indignation. The congressman wrote back to explain that the personnel director had been quite right. He even sent along a teacher's pay scale to illustrate the point. Diane just had too much education and too much experience to be hired. She finally realized that was the reason she was unable to get a teaching position in the previous state. She wished someone had been honest enough to tell her the reason.

Diane's story is not unique. Hundreds of women tell basically the same story. Some school districts are up-front with their applicants, some are not, but it is a fact not restricted to any particular geographical area, that experienced teachers who are mobile are not hireable. Good quality teachers, who have proved themselves in the classroom are simply not being hired, forcing their careers to end. Not only do the individual teachers suffer in such cases, but in the long run, America's children pay the price. Most experienced teachers would agree that even third and fourth year teachers are not as well equipped for teaching success as proven, experienced teachers. Still, these professionals are being turned away from our nation's classrooms every year for only one reason - money. Teacher pay scales vary widely from state to state, but all give monetary credit for each year or two of teaching experience. The compensation for each step ranges from just a few hundred dollars to several thousand. Districts have found that one of the easiest ways to keep within their budgets is to hire inexperienced teachers, thereby saving on teachers' salaries.

Teachers who graduate from 'top' schools get no more consideration than those who graduate from marginal schools. In fact, those who graduate from 'good' schools seem to get less consideration. Not only is experience a detriment to teachers, advanced degrees and extra graduate units are also a major factor in determining the hireability of job-seeking teachers. Teacher pay scales generally add pay steps for graduate units toward an advanced degree, a Masters and/or a Doctoral Degree. Applicants with the most education are the least likely to be hired. Teachers are not hired because they have received good grades, good recommendations, high test scores, higher degrees or for their success in the classroom. Teachers are hired using only one criteria - cost! It is often heard from administrators that 'new' teachers are hired over 'old' teachers because new teachers are more proficient with the latest teaching methods, techniques and materials, but nothing can make up for experience. This explanation is only a rationalization of an unpalatable policy.

Teachers like Diane, who relocate often in our increasingly mobile society also suffer from other abuses. Each state has its own standards for teacher certification, and each college or university has its own teacher programs. Most of these schools are state certified and, therefore, educate their future teachers according to legal requirements in the state in which they are located. Not only does certification vary from state to state, but there is also little flexibility or interstate cooperation in behalf of the certified teacher. Being certified in one state does not assure certification in the next. Most often, some sort of test or added course must be taken with each new application, and these are frequently repetitious.

To compound the difficulties, certification requirements are constantly changing within each state. Frequently, this means education majors have to take additional courses and delay graduation just to keep up with the changing state requirements. Working teachers also must to keep up with each new requirement. In one of the western states, a law was passed requiring a master's degree for all teachers, tenured or not, within five years. In this particular state, only three universities offered acceptable master's programs, so many teachers had to drive hundreds of miles to get to an appropriate school. Some drove back and forth in the evening and some spent their summers away from home in order to take a needed classes. Both methods created family and economic problems within the home. After less than five years this law was dropped and all the heartache was for naught except a few extra dollars in salary per year.

It would be impossible to go through the various changes within each state's teacher certification program over the last forty years. Some of the changes have been brought about by the teachers' organizations, usually as trade-offs for higher wages or improved working conditions. Some of the changes were and are still made in hopes of improving teachers. In the long run, all of these are abusive. There are very few 'grandfather clauses' for teachers. If a district or state decides to change the law, all teachers, old or new, must re-qualify or leave. States tend to make major changes at least every five years and many, even more frequently.

Many states accept college degrees as sufficient proof of competency to receive teaching certification. A late addition to teacher certification requirements across the country has been a variety of teacher competency tests. In order to qualify for certification, teachers must pass a test unique to that state with a required score. Acceptable scores vary from state to state. A large percentage of the states, although not all, require the National Teacher Exam. Some states accept only their test. Some states will accept a stated percentage scored on the Graduate Record Exam, but not all. Each certification applicant must take that state's particular test, whether they have no teaching experience or twenty years of teaching experience, and whether they have taken and scored high enough on the NTE or the GRE or any other state exam not honored in the new state.

The abuse in this case lies in requiring all teachers, whether experienced or recent graduates, to take the test. These tests became law, and/or came to be accepted because of the general belief that teachers are not competent, even in basics and that their education does not qualify them to teach. Teachers should be accepted as able to teach our children because they have graduated from accredited colleges or universities. We are attacking the wrong end of the problem. As we will see in the next chapter, the best qualified teachers in the world (or the most rigorously tested) will not be the answer to raising student performance, which presumably is the goal toward which we are striving. The testing policies described above are abusive to teachers and reinforce the false premise that has permeated our nation that teachers are the cause of poor student performance.

Another irony which recently surfaced in our country which is so concerned about having 'good' teachers, is the early retirement policy. In some states teachers are given incentives for an early retirement and due to teacher abuses, many are taking advantage of that. This type of policy came into being for only one reason – money. The purpose of the policy is, of course, to get rid of the experienced, well educated teachers that we profess to be seeking in favor of unseasoned, newly certified teaching personnel to reduce salaries.

Mrs. Anderson
Mrs. Anderson taught in an inner city school for several years before the school was closed due to a large drop in the school age population and she was transferred to another school. Mrs. Anderson was happy with the new school, but it was a long way from her home. Therefore, she asked for a transfer to a school nearer to her home and received an offer to teach in a new government program. She taught in this special program for three successful years before she was told her contract would not be renewed. The government program paying her salary was being terminated. Her principal felt badly about the situation, but had no other position to offer Mrs. Anderson. She waited all summer, applying for each new job that became available, but because of a loss in students in the district, several teachers including Mrs. Anderson were not rehired.

Two prominent changes that have taken place during the past 50 years are the constant shift and decline in the school age population, and the growth of federal government influence in our public schools. These two major factors have brought about many monumental changes in the system and many of these have had a direct effect on teachers.

Financially, school systems are dependent on many different tax sources for income and are never sure what funds will be available from one year to the next. States have also limited the amount each district can spend per child in each school in an effort to equalize the educational opportunities in each school district. This has only made the situation worse, as the more affluent parents now contribute to their local schools to provide the extras (many provided as standard curriculum in the past). Poorer parents are still left with more poorly equipped schools and no way to improve the situation. Many federal programs have been added to local school curricula. Usually, a special federal program will require certain specifications be met by the various schools before the money is forthcoming and reporting as it is implemented. This can be justified in the short term, but the money might not be available for the same program the following year, necessitating a new source of funds to continue the program, or, if none are available, dropping the program altogether. Some districts simply do not have enough money to keep the teachers they have and must let regular teachers go as well. All this uncertainty is hard on both teachers and students.

Some of the federally funded programs have been effective or a step in the right direction. Most however, are more societal in nature, rather than educational programs, such as school breakfast and lunch, bilingual programs and early learning. Often, they result in added duties for teachers already teaching a regular class. The funding and execution of these programs can be very complex and since most are mandated by the federal government, must be implemented exactly as specified, requiring extra administration. Teachers are sometimes caught in the middle and lose their jobs, while regular classroom teachers are asked to do a lot of additional work, with no extra pay.

Mrs. Jones

Mrs. Jones has taught third grade at the same school for fifteen years. For the last three years she has been required to remain in her classroom one hour after school is out to remain with the children in her room who take the 'late' bus. These children take the 'late' bus because there are too few buses in the district to transport all the children, so some buses must do double shifts at each school. When Mrs. Jones first started teaching third grade at this school she had children in the classroom from eight in the morning until four in the afternoon, an hour to two longer than other schools. Due to the transportation problem, her school was chosen to teach longer days so the buses could take children home from another school first. Each year the time schedule changes for one transportation reason or another. Mrs. Jones has found that she has to plan additional activities for her children in order to keep them from getting too tired. She and her students are wilted at the end of the day. The parents were told that the longer hours are good for the students because it gives them a chance to strengthen their academic foundations, but Mrs. Jones knows the real reason for the longer hours and that the students aren't learning any more. In fact, some are too tired to learn much at all. Mrs. Jones' case is representative not only of the transportation problems many schools have, but that outside situations can affect classroom performance of both students and teachers.

As a new teacher in the 60's, I never gave a thought about guns, much less about gun violence in our schools. While there were school shootings in our history, it wasn't something students or teachers worried about. The first time I had a personal experience with guns in school was when I was teaching in an elementary school in Southern California. My class was 'self-contained,' remaining in my classroom all day. The district policy was that any student bringing a gun to school would be expelled. However, I was

40

asked to take a student into my classroom who had brought a gun to his 6th grade class in another school. The rationale was that he was a good kid who had made a mistake, but he hadn't intended any harm to anyone with the gun. I took the student, and he did well, but I still think to this day that it was abusive to ask that of me and the other students in my class.

I had an 8th grade homeroom class one year in which a male student, known to be a probable gang member, was one of my students. One day, as I was walking up and down the aisles checking on work, I noticed this student was wearing a young girls 'cartoon characters' watch. I asked this student why he was wearing it, as he always wore gang member attire, and he told me it was because he was 'carrying.' I just said "oh," and continued my walk. For some reason it didn't really scare me, but when the students left at the end of the period I reported what had happened to the office and I never saw the student again. Another student in that same homeroom brought a gun to school and accidentally dropped it on the office floor. He was sent home for a few days, but because he was a 'Special Education' student, there was no further punishment and he was in my homeroom for the remainder of the year.

Several lock downs occurred while I was teaching at a Middle School. Gun activity in the immediate area was the cause. There was an apartment building directly across the street from the school that had been taken over by a gang, and shots were fired into the parking lot area at the rear of the school, but they were usually ignored. If criminal activity was taking place nearby, the school would go on lock-down. Teachers were required to lock the classroom doors from the inside so that intruders couldn't unlock the doors from the hall or outside. The students remained at their desks, and no one was allowed near the windows. Normally, we didn't have any food or water in the rooms, and no one could leave to use the bathroom. One lock-down lasted until after dark on a rainy night, and a bolt of lightning hit an electrical box on a pole on the school grounds, sending sparks flying. It was loud and scary. The students understood what was going on and were quiet, and I believe they were frightened. I always tried to go on with the lesson as long as I could, but mostly I just let the students talk quietly, read, or draw during a lock-down.

I remember while driving home from school hearing about the Columbine Shootings on the radio. I was sure that after that horrific tragedy that something would be done about guns. I've had the same thought after each school shooting and I'm still wondering. In fact, I have been wondering for years why so many Americans have guns? I couldn't imagine why after Columbine, Sandy Hook, Parkland and all the other mass shootings that taken place in America, legislators, both state and federal, haven't done something to control the use of guns. During my research for this book I discovered the 'whys' and I find them very disturbing.

A former member of an Evangelical Christian Church provided me one reason. Evangelical Christians believe that the occurrences of all of the wars, epidemics and disasters that have been taking place in the world in last decade or so are signs that the time of Tribulation is upon us, and that what is now happening in Israel is bringing mankind close to the End of Times. Evangelicals believe that Obama is the Antichrist and would exorcise God and enslave the holy people when he was in office. Therefore, after Obama was elected, Evangelicals bought millions of guns to defend themselves from what Obama might do. Evangelicals strongly believe Trump is helping them in the struggle against the Antichrist, and that he is bringing them closer to Christ and the coming of Armageddon.

Other groups believe they too have good reason to have guns. White Supremacists still fear the blacks and have armed themselves in accordance. Hunters, and those who have an ancestral gun or two, add to the mix, and I am sure there are other gun owners with their own various reasons to have guns. Some members of the Right, as we have learned, might feel they need guns to protect themselves

42

from the government which they consider bad, and which burdens their corporations with disliked regulations.

The justification for owning guns, the 2nd Amendment to the United States Constitution, the Right to bear Arms states:

> "A well regulated Militia, being necessary to the security of a free State, the right of the people to keep and bear Arms, shall not be infringed."

The National Riffle Association, backs gun owners by lobbying the legislators of both our state and federal governments to eliminate all gun control legislation, and contributes enormous amounts of money to get pro-gun candidates elected. The NRA receives large donations of money from the Right, and from gun manufacturers to use for that purpose.

A consequence of having a well armed segment of our population has been the massacre of hundreds of innocent Americans in mass shootings, some taking place in our public schools. Many children are traumatized and afraid to go to school. Teachers, too, have been victims of these mass shootings and are also afraid. Instead of attacking the root of the problem, that of too many guns in the hands of civilians, our leaders from the local to the national level choose to handle the problem by teaching our students and teachers how to handle the gunmen when they invade our schools and arm the teachers so that they can help protect the students. This has got to be the ultimate form of disrespect for both our teachers and our children.

Reasons

Societal and demographic changes have made a marked change in both students and teachers. Students are not as prepared or motivated as they were in the past. Society's expectations are that different teaching methods and changed teacher qualifications will raise test scores. Parents have abdicated their responsibilities and expect teachers to become de-facto parents, teaching students unprepared to learn.

When I began teaching in the early 1960's, teachers across the nation were not paid much more in comparison with teachers are today, yet teaching was considered a respected and worthwhile career. Teachers were also considered good credit risks; even young single teachers, had no trouble buying a car or leasing an apartment. One was proud to be a teacher and a respected member of the community. If teachers in comparison are not paid a great deal less now, why has the attitude toward teachers changed so drastically? There is much more to a teacher's loss of community respect than just a loss in purchasing power. Society has changed its attitudes and values dramatically in the last fifty years, and teachers are victims of the great social changes to a greater degree than the personal financial loss.

To be considered upper class prior to the 1960's one had to have money, family, education, culture and all the lifestyle trappings that went with appearing in social columns and events. The 1950's movie "High Society" exemplified this group. The Kennedy family, even though they had most of the requirements to be upper class, were always reminded that they had achieved it except for 'family'.' Their ancestors were not quite acceptable to 'real' high society. There were very few newcomers to the upper class. The 'new rich' were not a part of the true upper crust. There was a great middle class, the category most people considered theirs. To be a member of the middle class you had to have a reasonable amount of money, usually coming from a good job. There was a wide span of incomes included in the middle class bracket. Most professionals, including doctors, lawyers, engineers and businessmen were at the top; teachers, civil servants and small businessmen were in the middle, while skilled labor was at the bottom of this class. The amount of money one made did not automatically put individuals in the certain subgroup within this large denomination. As in the upper class, family, education, culture and personal possessions all contributed to one's place in this strata.

Teachers were respected within this middle class society because they had a good education and were considered cultured and respectable. These qualities were esteemed equally with money. But the one thing that set this middle class apart from the other two classes was a strong sense of ethical and moral values. Certain standards of social behavior were expected from middle class people and most class members adhered to these standards publicly, if not in fact. Again, teachers scored high in the standards department. Most were considered above reproach. If a teacher feared for his or her job in that era, it was usually because they had strayed in one way or another from middle class standards, and not because of incompetence as no one dared question a teacher's professional integrity. Striving for excellence was very much a part of this value system, and anyone who reached the top in his/her profession was well regarded. The lower class consisted of the very poor, most minorities and those who refused or were unable to adhere to middle class morals. Entertainers and other flashy public figures usually lived on the fringes, not accepted by either the middle or upper classes because of background or unusual lifestyle.

The American class system is now structureless. Today, status in our society is based primarily on wealth. All other indicators of status are no longer valid. Globalization is another factor to consider when talking about class. The billionaires of the world now form a global class of their own. The members of this class do business all over the world. Their primary loyalty often goes to the fellow members of this unique class rather than to their own country.

The sixties and seventies brought about a great social upheaval. The flower children of the sixties, the Vietnam War, integration, the media revolution, mobility, women's liberation and the increasing power and influence of the federal government were all movements that helped bring about enormous change in our society. These times saw the disappearance of social columns from newspapers - an outward sign of the new generation's disdain for tradition. Living together, having children out of wedlock, an ever-increasing divorce rate became examples of the disappearance of the old middle class standards, no longer respected. Youth was worshiped and aging scorned. It was not only young people that changed, as it was suddenly alright for a clergyman, politician, or other public figure to be divorced and still keep their position. Slovenliness became a fashion trend and it slipped into other areas as well. Social 'dropouts' became so common they became socially acceptable. Homosexuals came out of the closet. Women's clubs and social functions of all types were no longer important. The 'flower child' generation turned into the 'Me' generation whose thinking brought even more change. Responsibilities were thrown to the wind and self-gratification became the reason for living. Striving for excellence and self-sacrifice were no longer revered. Later came Generation X and now the Millennials. The Baby Boomers, those born from approximately 1946 through 1964, were the instigators of the vast changes. Those who followed have been living in the wake of those changes. They have never known other way.

The Vietnam War was one of the causes of this new thinking. The reason for the fighting was as obscure as the country itself to most of the nation. Young men whose fathers had so gallantly gone off to World War II, fled to Canada to avoid the draft. Students protested not only the draft, but the war itself. For many, flag wavers became targets of ridicule. Our National Anthem was sung with less fervor. It seemed that our very nationalism was at stake as the old middle class value system disintegrated.

Another integral part of the complex and confusing changes during the same period was the attempted integration of the black community into the mainstream, or more exactly, into the middle class of American society. Most who are living now do not realize what monumental attitudinal changes had to take place within the middle class for us to come as far as we have with this enormous task. Only a few years ago, if a black family moved into an all-white neighborhood, the neighbors would immediately put their homes up for sale at the risk of large losses on the price, just to escape. This blockbusting furthered the creation of sprawling white suburbs surrounding our major cities and changed the living patterns of American families. Schools in many parts of the country became integrated for the first time and a great many private schools sprang up, especially in the South, to keep white children from having to attend the integrated public schools. Television shows and commercials began to feature blacks and school text books included blacks and other minorities in their illustrations for the first time.

Many gains have been made in the attempt to erase racism from our society, but beginning with the election of President Barack Obama in 2008 racist views began again gaining momentum, as seen in the violence toward blacks by the police, White Supremacists, many members of the public, and by the legislation that has curtailed voting rights. Other minority groups, such as the Chinese, Japanese, Vietnamese and other Asians, Hispanics, and some religious groups, such as Muslims are becoming victims of violence.

A brief history lesson might make the lingering and even newly erupting racism in our society, especially in the South more understandable. At the time our constitution was written, the southern states population was 50% black. Almost 100% of the black population in the South were slaves whose labor was necessary for sustaining the agricultural based economy of that region. Southern plantation owners could not survive without their slaves because they needed the labor force and slaves were valuable commodities on the open market. White slave owners were afraid of the threat of slave uprisings and violence against whites because there were so many of them. Owners kept slaves in their place by separating slave families and handing out extreme and cruel punishments for anything that might lead to any type of aggressive or threatening behavior. They were considered less than human by southerners, and by many others as well, as exemplified in the United States Constitution stating that Blacks counted as only 5/8 of a human being.

Today, blacks make up less than 13% of the total population of the United States, making them one of the smallest minority groups in our country. Mounting any type of a threatening force would be very difficult for them, even if they had the desire to do so. Yet, the two concepts, the extreme fear that the slaves could and would cause great harm to whites if they were freed, and the belief that blacks are not fully human, are still held by some of America's citizens today, as exemplified by the violence toward blacks that has been escalating in all areas of our country. Perhaps the understanding of this part of our history, upsetting as it is, can help us to solve some of the problems we now face.

The work to integrate our minorities into the mainstream of our society has been going on for many years and will continue. Tax supported employees such as teachers and other civil servants plus large monopolies such as the Bell System were among those given hiring quotas for minorities. The entertainment world became a highly integrated segment of our society. It is sometimes hard to remember that before the 1960s black groups had not begun to emerge on the public/entertainment scene and black singers recordings were not yet on the jukebox except in predominantly black areas. It was not that long ago that Martin Luther King marched on Washington. Fifty years is not very long for a society to make such basic human rights adjustments, and now we, as a nation, seem to be losing the progress that so many worked so hard to achieve in this area.

If, for any reason, a group had not received equal opportunities in the past, rules were changed or bent to make up for these past inequities. Many major universities changed both entrance and graduation requirements to enable those who had lagged to take advantage of the new opportunities. Many of these policies have now halted or been reversed, but the impression they made on the public still lingers. Some groups of white people, especially the uneducated and poor, adhere to the belief that white people are superior to other races, and therefore any achievement made by non-whites must have occurred because the non-white achiever took the place of a white person who was obviously more qualified. Members of our society who were in their forties or older when the enormous changes were taking place are now seventy plus and are declining in number. But, we must keep in mind that integration and the other societal changes came after their formative years. Therefore, we cannot fault them for hanging on to some of their childhood values.

During the 1960's and 1970's two very distinct political groups, with very divergent views of government and outlook on life, began to coalesce into the two groups that we now call Conservatives and Liberals, Right and Left, and much less accurate, Republicans and Democrats. I will refer to these two groups as the Right and the Left.

The movement toward the Right was begun by a group of very conservative and very wealthy corporate leaders who didn't like the changes taking place in American society. Their philosophy's basic tenets are as follows: The members of the wealthy elite of American society should determine the direction society takes. For this, they deserve the praise and devotion of the remainder of the population. Those not within the elite must adhere to the constitution and other laws (as interpreted by the elite), while it is permissible to maintain their power through the use of violence and cheating. They consider governments a nuisance because governments place regulations on corporations that restrict wealth. They also believe that safety and well being of the public takes second-place to wealth accumulation, that our country's natural resources are unlimited, that climate change isn't real, that conservation of our lands and waters is not necessary

The elite Right kept their platform and plans a secret from the public. They formed political action groups with very patriotic sounding names to begin the implementation of their political goals. The Right's agenda resembles the following:
- Pay little or no taxes, personally
- Bring back segregation
- Close our borders to all immigrants
- Eliminate all civil rights
- Destroy the public school system
- Destroy Social Security
- Destroy Medicare and Medicaid
- Provide complete freedom for corporate actions
- Eliminate public protests and free speech
- Eliminate any type of government regulations on any sector of industry or business
- Advance the war industry by purchasing provisions of war from private for profit businesses
- Make guns available to everyone without regulation
- Establish Evangelical Christianity as the official religion of the United States

The Lefts' views are quite different from the Right's:
- The United States Constitution is still the foundation of our government.
- Governments' job is to protect all of our citizens from corporate activities that put peoples lives or health in danger, or harm our environment.
- Civil rights are for all people, no matter their gender, race, religion, age, or social standing.
- They support a strong public school system.
- They want to retain Social Security and Medicare. A large percentage of the Left support Universal Health Care.

- War should be limited to defensive actions and approved by the congress of the United States. No individual should profit financially from any war.
- They believe in gun control.
- Life, liberty and happiness should be a possibility for all American Citizens.
- They support a fair and adequate tax plan.
- Church and State should be completely separate.

Public schools are the battle ground between the philosophies of the Right and the Left. The progress each side has made toward meeting their own goals for molding our government to their beliefs can be seen everywhere in our society. The condition of our present day public school system is one of the biggest indicators of where each side stands.

The influence of the Right since the 60's has caused the public's perception of teachers to change - not the teachers, themselves. Since the amount of money anyone has amassed or earns is today's indication of success, teachers are portrayed as failures and should not be respected. Teachers still have the same amount of education, work just as hard, or harder, care very much for their students, and for the majority, turn out good students. The Right's campaign to undermine teachers, and thus our educational system, has used school integration plus the influx of mainly Hispanic immigrants to prove the negative effect on our childrens' education by blaming teachers for all of educations woes. For years, the Right has been fostering bad publicity about poor teaching and the decline of our public schools. The constant supply of negativity about the quality of our teachers and schools has been effective. School teachers have lost the respect of the public and their support. Tax payers don't want to support immigrant or less desirable students or poor students whose parents don't pay taxes. Some older people don't want to pay for the younger generation's children; they did their duty for their own. Government officials who shout "No new taxes" especially for schools, have been elected again and again by a public that sees less reason to support our public schools.

Professions other than teaching are suffering from the phenomenon of money worship. Lawyers are one of the first groups to come to mind. Their secret is out. There is an oversupply of lawyers and the average income of a new lawyer is lower per year than that of a teacher. They also receive lower ratings on the respect scale. The one thing that saves a lawyer from complete social ostracism is the fact that many lawyers do eventually achieve financial success; since their paychecks are not public knowledge, no one is sure which lawyer has the money and which one only plays the part. Teachers are not so lucky, as anyone who is interested can determine teacher pay scale in a particular district merely by asking. Teachers have become the victims of a deliberate and planned movement to destroy our public schools. It is more than just the low salary that has caused the teacher to lose society's respect. Teacher salaries have always been low. It is the fact that the Right has convinced the general public that only those with money deserve respect. Because teachers lack money, they lack respect. Today's teachers lack respect both on and off the job.

Teachers aren't the only middle class group being threatened by economic problems such as job insecurity, uneasiness about federal programs like Society Security, concern about retirement plans and medical benefits, the loss of industry to foreign countries, the rapid growth of some minority populations, the inability to buy homes and in general a loss of hope. For the first time in American history, the present generation cannot expect to live better than their parents. But instead of supporting the one system that can bring renewed vitality to the middle class, the system of public education, the middle class is attacking and locking out this one ray of hope. A decline in the educational process can only mean a further decline in the middle class.

Along with the ever increasing public attacks on teachers, there are ever increasing responsibilities the public is heaping upon our schools and the teachers. This is done in hope that the image in the mirror will change. As we will see, the burden of implementing the Civil Rights Amendment, sex education, health education, meeting nutritional needs, family counseling and religion in the schools, are just a few of the programs that are now under the educational umbrella. The image in the mirror cannot change to reflect the 'old' America that existed before the 60's. 'Old America' no longer exists. Again, it does not make sense to destroy the one institution that, more than any other single factor, was responsible for the rise of the middle class, and which remains the one big hope of the middle class.

Adding 'insult to injury', teachers have not only lost their classroom autonomy, job security, pay raises and public respect, they are being blamed for the poor student performance. Is poor student performance the fault of the teacher? No. The past fifty years of record-setting changes have also affected the student who, along with parents, must assume some, if not most, of the responsibility for their lack of education. Today's students have many more problems than those of the 50's. This phenomenon should not be 'dumped' on teachers. A wide range of social changes, which also changed students' lives are identified here by the use of some case studies gathered over the years in conversations with various teachers, parents and students themselves to illustrate how society has affected students:

Amy

Amy is an intellectually gifted fifth grade student who is doing very poor work. The teacher knows that Amy's parents have recently gone through a divorce, but according to Amy's mother, Amy is adjusting to her new situation very well and is able to see her father regularly. What the teacher doesn't know is that the mother has started to date another man and is gone nearly every night as well as on weekends. Amy, at age ten, is left alone for hours on end. Most of the time her mother comes home after midnight, sometimes not until the early morning. Amy doesn't tell her mother that she is afraid to go to sleep alone and therefore she gets very little rest. She also doesn't eat properly because her mother rarely prepares dinner. The new man in her mother's life doesn't like the fact that Amy even exists, and the mother chooses to neglect her daughter in favor of the new love. Amy is very bright and understands what is happening, but that doesn't make her feel any better. She is very lonely and insecure. She wonders what will happen to her if her mother marries this new man. Her real father, she knows, doesn't want her either.

The divorce rate in the United States is extremely high and still rising. Unfortunately, a great majority of these divorces involve children. There have been many studies done and books written about the effect of divorce on children - there are so many ramifications the break-up of the family unit has on the children. The point is that students from broken homes have a wide range of problems which almost always affect their school performance. Teachers have no control over a student's family life and can do very little about the problems a student brings with him/her from home. Parents, administrators and counselors who say this is not true are setting up unrealistic and unobtainable goals for the classroom teacher. To put it another way, it is not the teacher's responsibility to solve domestic problems, nor should it be. Teachers should go out of their way to be understanding, and in most cases they are. But, teachers cannot assume the parents' responsibilities as well.

Gary

Gary, age nine, plays video games from the time he gets home from school until late at night. His sister, age fourteen, comes home from school each day and stays on social media until she decides it is time to eat, or even do homework, then returns to her phone.. The family has three large screen television sets hooked up to cable so that the parents can view their shows and the children can watch what they want. Family members spend at least six hours a day in front of the television and have been known to binge-watch a continuous twenty-four hours. Neither child gets very good grades but the parents are not concerned. Neither parent finished high school and they are doing just fine. They can afford three color televisions, can't they?

Americans now in their late sixties and older, grew up when television was in it's infancy. My family didn't have a television set until I was 8 years old. Before we had TV, my parents, my brother and I spent our evenings reading, listening to the radio, playing card and board games, discussing topics of interest, and learning each others' views about a myriad of topics, including religion and philosophy of life. I remember writing about my first personal philosophy of life at about 14 years of age. We always ate dinner together. Most American families at that time spent their evenings in much the same way.

Over the last fifty years, as television programming (and more recently, video gaming) proliferated, more family time was spent in front of the television set and less on their former pursuits, such as reading, playing card and board games, and having family discussions. Evenings began to consist almost entirely of watching television with only some reading and some playing. By the time these children, who are now 65+ were grown, everyone had at least one black and white television, and television had become a major force of change in American society.

Not only have we gone through a social revolution in our country over the last 50 years, we have also gone through a media and technical revolution. We now have large screen color televisions, personal computers and smart phones. These devices bring entertainment and news in its many forms, not only into our homes, but into our cars, work and school environment, and everywhere we go. Technical devices and the programming they offer, now dominate our lives.

What we see and hear on our technical devices is what is now shaping our thoughts, how we use our time, our philosophy of life, and influence our behavior, our health, our human relationships, and what we perceive is important. This total domination of our lives by technical devices has taken a hold of our lives. The move toward technical domination of our lives has taken more than 50 years, but the speed of this process has accelerated in the past few years. Those most affected are our children.

Whether we believe television, computers and other electronic devices have done more good than harm to society, they definitely have had an effect on how students respond to a formal learning situation. Just ask any teacher! "Students do not know how to work by themselves." "Students are at a loss to know what to do if they finish their work early." "Students can turn external noise on and off at will, including the teacher's voice." "Students have to be entertained in order to hold their attention." These are only a few of the common comments heard from teachers. Administrators and parents reactions resemble the following: "A good teacher should be able to command the students attention." "Teachers should be able to adjust to the changing times and teach accordingly." "A teacher who complains about the students is just a poor teacher, or is "out of date," or "out of touch."

Our nation's teachers are expected to compete for our children's attention with the flashing images, continuous motion and action on 'YouTube' shown on their portable devices. Teachers also compete with professionally produced, multi-million dollar gaming and drama productions shown on our nation's movie, television and video screens, all of which are aimed at instant gratification and pure enjoyment, rather than stimulating thinking, and call for little or no physical effort or exertion. Teachers must further compete using only the normal teaching tools found in any classroom and their own abilities. How can one person, standing in front of the class, compete with the best and most expensive efforts of the entertainment world? This domination by technical devices has a major effect on student learning. Students so preoccupied by these outside influences do not make the effort to learn. Learning requires effort, work, commitment, and time set aside purely for the educational process in school and at home. A great many of today's students just aren't bothering to make the effort, but the teachers are being blamed for the students failures, not the student. Teachers are asked to perform superhuman tasks and be entertainers as well; parents and administrators do not focus on the students' diversion of attention and time. As students' problems continue to grow, the public has no answers except to blame teachers.

From the beginning of my teaching career I've had concerns about the effect of TV viewing on my students. Content is not the only aspect to be concerned about when watching TV. Sitting in one spot for hours on end, perhaps in a darkened room, eating snacks, and staying up late to watch a certain show can affect our children's health.

What causes me the most concern is the length of time an image appears on the screen. While reading, thinking, walking, talking, or doing almost anything else, an image may be viewed as long as it takes to comprehend it. While watching TV, movies, or videos, images constantly move, flicker, or change so fast that it is hard to comprehend all that is happening. I believe this might be one reason why my students' attention spans are short, and why they find it difficult to concentrate on more than very brief assignments.

When nightly newscasts began back in the late 50's, they were broadcast in black and white, had one or two newscasters who sat at a desk and read the news. The camera remained pointed at the newscasters without movement for several minutes at a time. The viewer had only to concentrate on what was said plus several field shots that lasted much longer than they do now. These broadcasts lasted 15 minutes.

Over the years, newscasts have added color, video clips of news events, reports of weather, sports, traffic, special reports and such. The format on the screen has changed from one picture at a time, to split screens, some times having as many as four or five simultaneous 'talking heads', action videos in others, and often unrelated streaming is shown along the bottom of the screen, plus a logo, date and time. While it may appear impossible for humans to digest all of the information being given at any one time, careful analysis would show that the actual news content is minimal and a substantial portion of the content is fluff, self-promotion and commercial content. Our brains just can't comprehend all the flickering, flashing, talking and other motion all at one time. This, I think, is affecting the ability of adults and children..all of us...to comprehend what is going on around us.

Jimmy

Jimmy does not have any clothes to wear to school, and he rarely eats. He lives with his mother, who is on public assistance, in one room in a decaying city neighborhood. He has never seen his father and does not even know his name. Sometimes an official of some sort will come to Jimmy's neighborhood to try to get Jimmy and others like him to come to school, but most of the time they do not go. Sickness, fear, and a lack of supervision keep Jimmy from the classroom. There is no reason he can see for going to school anyway.

Jenny

Jenny is a fifteen year old alcoholic. Both parents are doctors and are gone most of the time. Neither they nor her teachers are aware of the extent of Jenny's problem. She has the capability to be a good student, but does not respond to the classroom environment.

Mark

Mark has been in four different schools in five years. His dad's job takes the family from one end of the country to the other. Mark sees no reason to make friends or try for good grades as he will just have to start over again in a few months - in a new environment - where everyone else is already part of a group and he is always the outsider.

Jose

Jose does not speak English. He and his family are not citizens of the United States; they live in constant fear of deportation to Mexico. Jose, however, by the laws of the state in which he is residing, is entitled to attend public school. Because he is eleven years old, he is entitled to enter at the sixth grade level even though he can neither read nor write English. His teacher is bilingual, but does not have the time to spend individually teaching Jose enough English for him to function in any classroom environment, at any grade level.

The new mobility of our nation's population affects both teacher employment and student performance and behavior. Growing up in California in the 1950s, there were many children living in our community whose fathers were in the Military. They often moved and were known as 'Army Brats'. Everyone knew that an 'Army Brat' was a social misfit and the possessor of a certain 'different' personality, brought about by constant change. Children who are constantly moved are unable to make any lasting friendships or community ties, and aren't a part of school traditions. The curriculum of each new school is slightly different and social groups are already formed. These circumstances have an adverse effect on these students' school performance.

.

During the sixties and seventies, large corporations also began moving their personnel around the country as much, or perhaps more, than the military. In fact, it became desirable to be relocated as usually meant a promotion. The brightest and the best have been on the move for many years and we have strong evidence it has affected

60

their children. Each school has a slightly different curriculum and some classes offered in one school are not available in the next. Students subjected to relocation find they arc either ahead or behind their new classmates and always have to face the problems of making new friends and getting used to new places. Thus, 'Army (and Corporate) Brats' have become very common in our society.

The neighborhood school was a norm in America up to the 70'when the integration of our public schools became law. In some communities, home builders were required to set aside enough land for schools in each new home development. The baby-boom wave swelled the school age population causing classroom overcrowding and creating the need for many more teachers. The need for both buildings and teachers peaked in the 70's and there has not been a baby boom since. The combination of social, political and technical changes that have occurred since the 'boomers' were school age plus the decline in numbers of post-boomer school-age children has resulted in the slow, but constant, erosion of the neighborhood school concept. The shrinking demand for so many physical plants has also caused additional problems. The displacement of teachers and students is just one example. Mostly, the schools being closed are in the older, more urban areas, frequently in the minority and/or low income neighborhoods. Residents of these communities are upset and justifiably confused. They feel their children have been singled out and are victims of one more abuse. The displaced children who were bused to other schools to follow integration laws in the district couldn't understand why they were being sent further from home to a new neighborhood where they are expected to compete among strange peer groups with more affluent backgrounds. They also faced a new set of teachers and a whole new scholastic and social environment with sometimes insurmountable expectations.

Poor neighborhoods are not the only ones affected by the excess physical plant problem. The white flight to the suburbs and rapid growth of Sun Belt cities created a lopsided population problem.

Often, there were too many schools for the number of children in a district, many located in the wrong places, forcing districts to draw strange boundary lines to avoid overcrowding or under-enrollment. An example is that of one family that lived in the same middle-class neighborhood for several years, but their two daughters attended three different elementary schools. Now, they attend a different Middle School than their neighbors - all due to the fact that the school board would not approve building new schools where they were needed since they already had several schools which were greatly under-enrolled.

Desegregation and its implementation has been a major force in the breakdown of the neighborhood school. Neighborhoods were extremely segregated in the past and although some progress has been made in the desegregation, considerable segregation still exists. In order to integrate the schools, boundary changes and busing have been attempted as the answer to the problem. Some districts have gone to the magnet school concept where certain schools are designated as 'schools for the gifted' or other special programs, designed to attract non-minorities to these predominantly minority schools. More recently, most school districts have instituted open enrollments, allowing students within a district to attend any school within district they choose, and some districts even allow out-of-district students to attend their schools.

The immigration problem in the United States is very complex. To make it a bit more understandable, a review of immigration is in order: Prior to 1492, when Columbus 'discovered' America, Native Americans, or Indians, were the only inhabitants of both North and South America. They had inhabited the Americas for thousands of years. The Vikings visited North America in the 900's, and possibly had settlement or two in what is now Eastern Canada, but abandoned those settlements approximately 1050. The Chinese may have visited the West Coast of America in the past, but evidence is sparse. It wasn't until Columbus that substantial immigration to the Americas began. In order to make the time line more understandable, Christ was born 1500 years prior to this time, the boundaries of the present day European and Asian countries were completely different, and both Australia and New Zealand were unexplored and both had native populations.

Europe, at the time of Columbus, was experiencing a time of enlightenment, (Shakespeare lived from 1564 to 1616), and European countries were interested in expanding their horizons by exploring other parts of the world, mostly to add riches to their coffers. The Americas had great quantities of gold and silver and the Europeans wanted it. Thus, a great era of exploration and exploitation began that brought Spanish, Portuguese, English, French, Dutch, German and others to the "New World". The great migration to America had begun.

Starting in the early 1540's the Spanish claimed the lands that are now Mexico, Florida, Texas, Oklahoma, New Mexico, Arizona, California, parts of Utah, Colorado, and Wyoming. Spain sent soldiers and religious zealots to establish settlements and outposts to be used to spread religion among the natives, and to find treasure, mostly gold and silver. From approximately 1513 to 1848 (235 years), Spain occupied major parts of North America, building Missions from San Diego to north of San Francisco and in Arizona. Spain gave large land grants to Spanish Nobility. Santa Fe, New Mexico was the trade center located between Northern Mexico and Independence, Missouri. Spain also owned what we call the Louisiana Purchase until 1800 when it was purchased by France.

Texas gained its independence from Mexico in 1836 and became a state in 1845. The United States of America purchased The Louisiana Purchase from France in 1803. It wasn't until 1848 with the Treaty of Guadalupe Hildalgo that the United States annexed all or part of New Mexico, Arizona, California, Utah, Nevada and Wyoming. On the day the Guadalupe Hildalgo Treaty was signed, The United States of America grew by nearly one-third. Either

Spain or Mexico had ruled what is now almost a third of the United States for over 230 years.

Thirteen English Colonies were established along the Atlantic coast of North America between 1607 and 1732. These colonies were established to bring greater wealth to England and in some cases, to give the settlers a chance to escape religious persecution. These colonies, were geographically very small compared to the size of the Spanish held lands, but they were very significant to us because they became the United States of America with the ratification of Constitution in 1788.

The Russians colonized Alaska and the West coast of North America from 1732 to 1867 to increase their fur trade because fur-bearing animals were disappearing in Siberia. They established an outpost at Fort Ross in 1818, near Bodega Bay, in what is now in Northern California. Russian colonization in North America ended in 1867 when the United States purchased Alaska from them. Alaska became a state in 1959. My German ancestors sailed up the Mississippi river in 1830 and settled in Missouri.

The United states continued to grow toward the west, taking the land from the Indians, the French, the Spanish and the Russians by force, purchase or treaty until 1912, when Arizona became a state. This completed "The Lower 48."

We can expand on two different factors gained from the knowledge of how and when the United States established its current boundaries. The first one is culture, and the second one is time.

Culture, as defined as the behaviors, beliefs and characteristics of a particular social, ethnic, or age group, and differs from group to group. Religion and language are the biggest separators of cultures. Race is NOT necessarily part of the definition of culture, and culture is NOT part of government, but large segments of the citizens of the United States don't understand the relation of culture and government. As we have learned, the United States contains many cultures within its borders. Not understanding the difference between race and culture, and between culture and government is causing problems for the citizens of the United States.

Time is different to each age group and to those who study history, and those who don't. A young child believes a day is a long time, a teenager thinks a year is a long time, while senior citizens find ten years is hardly any time at all. A historical time-line of 100 years is very short. To understand why cultural issues are dividing our country, and how those issues have usurped our politics, recall that even 500 years is a relatively short time in human history. The English colonies were established between 1607 and 1732. It took 125 years for the English to establish their colonies in America, then another 56 years to ratify the Constitution and free themselves from England to become the United States of America. At that time, Germans made up a large part of the population of the new United States, as did a few Dutch, French, Native Americans, African slaves, and free blacks.

The Spanish began their colonization of America in 1513 and expanded their presence during that time to cover two-thirds of what is now the United States, ending their expansion in 1848. That is 335 years. Their culture remains in Mexico, as well as Central and South America. Russian colonies existed between 1732 to 1867, or 135 years. Native Americans and their culture extended back thousands of years before the 'European invasion.' All of these peoples spoke languages other than English.

English was only one of the languages spoken in those colonies that ratified the Constitution, but it became the language of the new government. As the United States expanded geographically, English became the de facto language of the governments of the new states and territories. Other languages, especially Spanish, remained the cultural language of the western territories. An 'official' language has never been codified into law. The immigrants who came through

Ellis Island spoke many different languages; succeeding generations of these immigrants usually learned to speak English. From the beginning of the settlement of English colonies to the present, English has been the language of the government, but literally hundreds of different languages were and are spoken in the United States. All but the Native American languages come from other parts of the world.

It both angers and amuses me when I hear English-speaking Americans shouting at people who speak other languages in public places in the US telling them to "go back to where you came from", or "go back to your own country". England, from the early 1600's to the early 1900's colonized Australia, New Zealand, parts of Asia, Africa, Canada and other parts of North and South America. Although the English have lost most of their Empire, their culture (remember language is part of culture), remains. That explains why English is now a world-wide language. The English language is not native to America, any more than Spanish or French. When an American English speaker yells "Go back to where you came from" to some one in America speaking a 'foreign' language, that person yelled at certainly has the right to yell the same thing back.

Culture is not part of government and government is not culture. They are two separate components of a society. Americans get culture all mixed up with government. Citizens of the United States, or those wishing to become citizens, or those seeking refuge, owe their allegiance to the government of the United States of America, but they should be free to practice their own culture. Children of many different cultures are taught in our public schools, and each student deserves an equal opportunity to obtain a good education.

Prior to the 1970's, most immigrants came to the US as families, by themselves or in small groups, and became integrated into society fairly rapidly. Immigrant children learned English in public schools, but often studied their native language and their native country's traditions in Saturday schools. In the 1970's, a flood of Mexicans, and some Central and South Americans immigrated to the US, especially into California and Texas. Public schools were expected to educate these immigrants just as they had educated immigrant children of the past. The numbers were so large that their arrival caused not only problems with schooling, but in housing, city services, jobs, culture conflicts, and much more. I can only cover how the immigrant explosion affected the public schools, especially in California.

Hispanic immigrants tended to settle in the same areas. Metropolitan Los Angeles became home to large numbers that settled in South and Eastern Los Angeles. Los Angeles County, Orange County, Riverside County and San Bernadino Counties were all greatly affected by the onslaught of this new population. Schools were especially impacted.

The schools in highly impacted areas couldn't handle the number of new students with the existing facilities. Some of this problem was solved by White flight to mostly White suburban areas, leaving more room for the new students, but more had to be done. The track system, previously mentioned, was one answer, as was shifting grades to different schools. The elementary schools, grades K-6, were the most impacted, so it was decided that the 6 grade would become part of the Jr. Highs, and these schools became Middle Schools. The 9th grade, formerly part of Jr. Highs would go to the least impacted high schools. Tax monies going to these schools became less, as the neighborhoods in which these schools were located were declining, and school supplies dwindled. Up keep of school buildings was unaffordable.

Traditionally new immigrant students are enrolled in age appropriate grades, and this continued with the new immigrants as well. However, the situation was very different than that of the past. Normally there might have been two or three immigrant children in a class, but with this new situation entire classrooms would contain non English speakers. In fact, entire schools contained only non

English speakers. This had never happened before, and finding answers as to how to deal with this crises caused anger, bewilderment, frustration, and more in the teaching ranks.

One answer to the language problem was to hire bilingual teachers to teach K-3 in their native Spanish. This was done because research shows that children learn a new language far faster, and better, if they already read and write in their native language. At the 4th grade level the children would be taught in English only classes. Those students who were already in the upper grades would learn in classes taught by ESL (English as a Second Language) certified teachers.

There were not enough bilingual teachers to cover the classes, so other teachers were lured into learning Spanish with the promise of extra pay for becoming bilingual teachers. This did not sit well with many teachers. Just like those in the general population, some teachers didn't feel they should have to learn a new language to serve immigrant children. Many experienced English only speaking teachers were forced to change grade levels, find a job in a new new district, quit, or retire.

The predominantly Spanish speaking schools had Spanish speaking faculties, and often times Mexican sympathizers. In a K-6 school where I was teaching in the late 80's and early 90's, I was told by a young Mexican American teacher during a discussion about the impact Mexican immigrants were having on our country, that I should just learn to live with less. At this same school we had an annual day to celebrate our culture. One year I had my class do line dances in cowboy costumes, and sing patriotic songs, such as God Bless America. The majority of the classes did Mexican dances and songs, and waved the Mexican flag. Several teachers waved the Mexican flag and yelled "Viva Mexico" during the program. One of the teachers asked me after the program was over, if I wasn't afraid I was going to get in trouble for my classes' part in the program. I said no, but I wasn't sure I wouldn't be. This was in Southern California around 1990.

The "immigration crises" as I now call it is over. The attitudes of the teachers at the schools I have mentioned have changed as they have become more Americanized. The number of immigrant children in the neighborhoods where these school are located is way down. The schools where I taught are now back to normal one track schedules. But there are many visible lasting effects of the crises in our society. California's schools lost status compared to schools in other states. Some of California's communities were forever reshaped. We as a nation still have immigration, but it isn't a crippling problem. California is now the 5th largest economy in the world, and America's farmers need immigrant labor to harvest their crops, and many other industries depend on immigrant labor to ensure their success. Hundreds of thousands of immigrants have melded into American society contributing the talents and hard work, and pay a considerable amount of taxes.

The Right, however, has used immigration and it's problems to help convince the public that America's public schools are failing. Yes, the test scores from schools with predominantly immigrant students do have lower test scores, but these schools are not the majority of schools, and as we have seen, there are other reasons why America's schools are in trouble. Many of the problems as we have seen are actually caused by the Right.

Texas, Arizona, New Mexico have been highly impacted by Hispanic immigration, but every state in the nation has some immigrants, and just like California the public schools have shouldered much of the responsibility for their integration into American society.

In the late sixties, a friend taught history in a Middle School in a small town in the panhandle of Texas. At that time she taught six classes, five of them mostly white, the sixth having a few blacks, some Mexicans who were children of migrant workers plus some poor whites. This was the way the classes during that time were set up - the point is, that in 1969 the school was more than ninety-five percent white. She still has family in that town although she has not lived there for many years, and she keeps track of what is going on in their schools. Now, that same Middle School is well over fifty percent Mexican-American. This is due to the number of migrant workers who have become permanent residents and the decline in white residents. This type of enormous population shift is having staggering effects on our schools. It has affected both teachers and students, adding a sense of insecurity to both groups and greatly disrupting the learning process.

A percentage growth of the elderly and childless population has accompanied the shift in ethnic makeup of the American population. We now have a much larger percentages of people over sixty-five. Even though the elderly were very supportive of the schools when their children were of school age they now have different concerns and priorities and vote accordingly. The increases in childless couples and singles since the late fifties and early sixties has also resulted in a group who have different interests and give their support to other issues more pertinent to them. Thus, the schools and teachers have lost the support of a significant portion of the citizenry.

Whether the cause is parental guilt or some other factor, there appears to be denial that the enormous volume of working mothers has much to do with the way their children perform in school. Yet, how can we possibly think that the major change in the family structure that has occurred has no effect on the school performance of our children? In 1960, a small percentage of mothers with children under the age of eighteen worked outside the home. By 1980, that number had increased considerably; now it is the norm for mothers to work. Many people take for granted that once a child is in Middle School, he/she is grown up enough to take care of himself - that a mother's (or parent's) guidance is not a needed feature of after-school, or in many cases, before-school life. It is healthy for children to be able to share their school life with their family, especially their mothers. Elementary schools often have a

70

small clique of the "lucky" or affluent mothers who run the schools, while the working mothers can do very little. The children are very aware of whose mother spends time at school and whose is rarely there. This might have a greater effect on our children's school performance than we realize.

This brings up another point. The reason most mothers work is because the family needs the extra income or the mother is a single parent. In some cases, she has a profession she wants to fulfill, or perhaps she just enjoys working outside the home. The added income helps buy the multitude of material possessions our children and their parents believe they need to have to be an integral part of today's society. As we have discovered, money is the principal way Americans have of judging where they belong on the social scale, thus, parents as well as children have come to believe working mothers are a necessity — far more important than having her at home after school, or having her help out at school. Considering the current situation, they may be right, but we can't blame the teacher for this social decision that affects student performance. Another point to consider is that the non-working mother has joined the community's elite since it usually means that the husband must have a large earning capacity and she does not have to go to work — this is just another 'put-down' for the less affluent mother and her children.

Children of working mothers are called on to do many of the household chores, often taking on added responsibilities such as responsibility for younger siblings. Today's children are often treated more as adults than children, and they frequently carry responsibilities and worries formerly left to adults and far greater than a child should have to cope. This must have some effect on their learning ability.

One teacher discovered not long ago that there was only one child in her class of twenty-five children who lived with both natural parents. Another discovered that only seven children in her class of about twenty-five shared the current family name of their parents. One little boy was the only black child in his family of five. His mother had been married three times; once to a white man, then to a black man and then to another white man. In another class, the father of one of the children was in jail while another student's father had been murdered. Carol's father has been sexually abusing her since she was eight; she is now thirteen. Tom's mother put his hand on a hot burner one day to punish him for being bad. Susan always wears long pants and long sleeve shirts to cover up the welts and bruises she receives from regular beatings. Jim's father makes snide and disparaging remarks about teachers all the time (i.e., Jim shouldn't have to do much of anything the teachers demand — who do they think they are, anyway?)

Of course, not every student in every class has the problems mentioned in the preceding paragraphs, and some schools have more children with problems than others, but there are more children with such difficulties than we as a nation want to admit. The fact is that a large portion of our school age children are sent to school in such a state that learning for them is almost impossible. Teachers aren't able to learn for a student. Learning is a mental process controlled by the individual. A teacher can teach, presenting materials in many different ways, but no learning can occur unless the student is both able and wants to learn.

The medical profession has made great strides in the last fifty years toward lowering the infant mortality rate and keeping children with major health problems alive. Nothing but praise and admiration can be given the doctors and their achievements. One of the results of this medical progress is that an increasing proportion of disabled students are being placed in classes with the non-disabled at the same grade level. While we should provide for the disabled, this 'main-streaming' practice is often disruptive. The extra attention given to the disabled robs other students of classroom time. Prior to the 60's, most classes were tracked according to academic ability; disabled children were taught in a special, and separate, track. As discussed in another chapter, school performance is often judged by the state on average scores in standardized exams without regard to student ability. While not a major effect, main-streaming has contributed to lower exam scores.

We often compare the performance of our students to that of students in other countries. Our students rated near the bottom of the list in math and about in the middle in language skills. While this is due in part to problems previously discussed, a very important factor in making such a comparison is not just comparing test results, but knowing who took the test. Most countries do not educate or attempt to educate their entire population through college level. Countries such as Japan, England, France, Germany, etc., only pick the best students to continue on to what would be the equivalent of our high school. Therefore, unlike our students, only the best take the tests and, not surprisingly, show the highest scores. For those students not going on to college, there are technical and specialized profession-oriented schools plus apprenticeship programs.

Finally, we must face the fact that not all students are capable of mastering even the basics. Not all want to, yet we are keeping our young people in school until (in most states) they reach the age of sixteen and/or complete eighth grade. Many systems now pass the underachiever through the grades and even through high school. It is common for state subsidies to be provided according to attendance. Therefore, it benefits the school to keep non-learners in school.

There has been a movement to encourage all high school graduates to go to college. Some of the reasoning is rooted in the belief that a college education ensures higher earnings (and status) - this has been reinforced by the (growing number of) for-profit colleges plus an industry providing student loans so that students who formerly did not have the financial means might now attend college, whether intellectually equipped or not. With more of our graduates now go on to college, a larger number of students are taking the S.A.T. test. A major reason S.A.T. test scores are dropping is the fact that more of the less-able students are taking the test. Although more students are entering college, it does not mean they are a smarter generation, but rather that just a higher proportion of all students are entering colleges and this has the effect of lowering the S.A.T. scores. Despite this inequity and the fact that there are still as many excellent students as there have always been, the weight of difficulties/problems shouldered by too many students is causing a decline in the quality of our country's education system from coast to coast.

Low pay, lack of respect and too many students who are not educable are three major setbacks for teachers. This combination of factors is externally discernible, readily understood and unrelated to low abilities. However, teachers have a great many internal problems which are not easily recognizable by the public - abuse by their administrators and politicians.

There are fine principals and other administrators in our public schools. These dedicated people are sensitive to both the teachers and the students. Their schools are well run, and working in such an atmosphere is quite rewarding. Unfortunately, these are exceptional cases. As previously mentioned, lack of respect for teachers is common among school administrators and politicians as well as by the general public. These groups are quite guilty of placing education's woes on the teachers, who get very little backing or help from the very people who should know better. The attitude of administrators toward teachers shows up in the internal functioning of our schools. Teachers are not given adequate lunch periods or breaks. Some teachers cannot even go to the rest-room during the day because their schools do not provide for such time. More than one school exists where teachers are given thirty minutes for lunch, seemingly enough time, except that the time period is broken up into three segments of ten minutes each, one of which is duty time! It is upsetting to even report that this is not unusual.

Over the past few years, the number of administrators in our system compared to both teachers and students has grown at an alarming rate. We can blame the federal government for much of this growth. The federal government assumed an enormous educational foothold when school integration became a federal responsibility. Numerous other federal programs over the years have also contributed to the federalization of our public schools. Many of these programs are partially or wholly financed by the federal government. Almost every program added to a school district's curriculum requires a new administrator to implement it. Public opinion has much to do with increased services, hence placing more administrators into the system. For instance, it is the public's opinion that electronic devises, such as computers, should be a made a part of every classroom. Many school districts across the nation have spent not only large amounts of money for the computers, but for administrators to run the programs, technicians to keep the systems running, and some districts have even added highly paid specialists to teach the classes. There are administrators to coordinate primary reading programs and administrators to coordinate upper grade reading programs. There are administrators to coordinate just about every subject, sub-subject and special program offered by the schools. This might sound good to most, but these administrators are highly paid, especially when compared to teachers, and are required for reporting as required in the law or mandate establishing the program. They are, for the most part, unnecessary. Their increase in number has done very little to raise the level of education in our classrooms and, in addition, they are taking away money from our teachers salaries as well as from provision of needed materials for the classroom.

These same administrators are often condescending and rude to teachers. These so-called specialists quite often make it so difficult for a teacher due to the paperwork and need for the specialist to prove that such a program might be needed by a student, that the teacher gives up trying to take advantage of what is offered. Thus, many students who should be getting this extra help, are not. School administrators rarely take a teacher's recommendation into account when implementing a program, when recommending students for a special program, or in its final evaluation. Teachers are well aware of their position within the structure itself. They are at the very bottom.

There are now far more female teachers than male. Some schools are finding it increasingly difficult to fill coaching positions and other traditionally male-dominated fields, simply because there are not enough male teachers to go around. Many schools are looking to the community to find part-time coaches, similar to Little League programs. Women have become the overwhelming majority in the teaching field and that in itself is causing problems. In our society where there are so many one-parent homes and that parent is usually a woman, a strong male influence is needed more than ever for both boys and girls. It is conceivable that a child can go through school and never have a male teacher, not even for physical education. This can become a grave problem and one that continually worsens, as so few college students, especially males, are going into education. We might ask, 'why is having a predominantly female work force a concern for the teachers themselves? Whether we like to admit it or not, women do not command the respect, nor do they have the power connected with a male work force.

Women teachers are not poor teachers, on the contrary, teachers are shown little respect in our society because they are poorly paid and this has nothing to do with ability. Low pay coupled with a lack of respect and power, have rendered teachers' organizations virtually useless. During negotiations, unless teacher groups promise to take more courses, or in some other way 'improve' their teaching, they have little chance of getting raises or other benefits. Teachers do not need nor should they make any more trade offs. Teacher groups are looked on as unions, rather than professional organizations. This is wrong. Teachers are not "labor" and administration and school boards management, yet much of the public and school boards, themselves, have this opinion. Instead, the teacher - administration - school board relationship should be viewed much like the doctor - hospital administration - Board of Directors relationship. Teachers, like doctors, are the professionals performing the institution's main business.

Many states have recently increased their teacher requirements. These changes came about as a reaction to what the public, as well as the administrators and politicians, perceive as the main problem of education, poor teachers and poor teaching methods. No one is altogether against the upgrading of teacher requirements, but it is doubtful that these moves are the answer nor will they have positive effects in the long run unless other vital changes are introduced. Ninety-nine percent of teachers have an undergraduate degree, and many of them have a Masters or even a Ph.D. Teachers are also aware that they, as a group, are doing a good job. But, it is apparent that neither the degree nor the effort seem to be enough. Not only is a degree required, but most states require teachers to continue their education as long as they are working in the field. Many states have another requirement - the degree must be earned within a specified period of time.

Continuing education in itself is not bad. When it is used as a punitive measure, perhaps for an offense not even committed, then it is bad. Teachers, who are not at all convinced they are the reason for poor student achievement, are being abused by states requiring higher certification — for no reward, appreciation, or better pay. Teachers are aware clerks, unskilled and semi-skilled labor, uneducated and those with much less responsibility/qualifications, are better paid - this does not set well.

It is unfortunate that in the past, teachers, through their various organizations, have brought much of this upon themselves. Over the years, as we have seen, teachers have been given raises and have added steps to their pay scales by bargaining, with the promise of continuing education. This has backfired. Pay scales are in no way compensatory to the amount of education most teachers have obtained, and the expense of earning the extra units or degrees far exceeds the rewards.

The amount of education that teachers are required to obtain should put them on an equal status with professional counterparts, however, teachers are treated as anything but professionals. A professional can set his/her own wage, choose his own hours and uses his/her education to perform particular duties in line with his/her education level. Furthermore, a professional commands respect for that unique knowledge and training, be it in law, medicine, electronics, etc. Teachers do not fit into any of these professional molds, yet educationally, there should be a professional category for them. This inconsistency, coupled with the other problem areas, is causing a devastating morale and emotional problem within the teaching ranks. Added educational requirements only add more frustration to the already smoldering chain of events.

Remember Diane, described in the previous section? We have many 'Dianes,' well educated women who are married to men who are rising rapidly in their careers and, therefore, tend to move around, or be moved around by the big corporations, more than the average family. This group of teachers will suffer even more because of the added teacher requirements, thus multiplying the frustrations and inability to be hired of this of this large group of trained, experienced teachers. These additional requirements have entrenched the policy of hiring new, inexperienced teachers at the expense of the students and our best, time-tested, teachers.

It is ironic that a society holding such a low opinion of teachers, indeed the entire system of education, would call upon this group to take on increasing responsibility for their children's development. Teachers are called upon not only to teach the basics plus any new topics that society might, at any time, deem necessary; they are also expected to teach moral and ethical values, health, sex, and other related topics and, in addition, provide before and after-school supervision, including, in many cases, two meals a day. At the same time, some religious groups want to reserve the teaching of morality and its trappings to the home environment, complicating both the majority's curriculum and forcing teachers to walk a fine line in the classroom.

With knowledge of the problems facing teachers, we should be anxious to resolve them. Will solving some of the problems help raise the standards of education? Since the root of education's woes is neither teachers themselves, nor poor teaching, the answer lies in taking a holistic view of the system and subsequently overhauling it to reflect the reality of today's society. However, if we do not do something specifically for teachers, we will soon have a shortage of qualified teachers that will surely cripple this nation's educational system. It should also be obvious that ending Teacher Abuse will also bring an end to some of the systematic educational problems.

Consequences

As the public education system deteriorates, a less educated populace is led to make poor decisions about ways to repair it.

The consequence of the intentional abuse and demeaning of America's teachers has caused Americas' public school system incredible pain. The most terrifying result of a poor education system is the creation of an under-educated and worse, an uneducated population. The uneducated are far more gullible than the educated, and tend to believe falsehoods because they are unfamiliar with facts, and lack an understanding of the history which has influenced the present. Uneducated people tend to make very poor decisions, and are causing enormous, and far reaching problems for our nation. President Trump has said many times that he loves the uneducated. Trump has convinced his base that education is bad. Thirty percent of women identifying themselves as Republicans now think that education is bad. This type of thinking is very destructive to a free and open society. The consequences of having a failing public school system are catastrophic, and affect every part of American society.

Every time I hear our traffic person on the local news tell us that traffic is going "slow" down the interstate, I want to stand up and yell "slowly" to the TV! If I actually did that, I would be constantly standing up and yelling at the television over grammatical errors made by our newscasters, both local and national. The gradual disintegration of correct use of the English language is showing up on every type of media, print and electronic, as well as in every day conversation. I hear things like "Me and her are going to the mall", "I wish I had went there" and other such grammatical errors every day.

Today's Americans rarely use anything other than electronic media to communicate. Just a few years ago, Christmas and other special event cards, friendly letters, and business transactions were communicated through the written word. It was very important to make sure that spelling, grammar, punctuation, and sentence structure were correct when communicating by the written word. Using electronic devices for communication has changed that. We still hear full sentences spoken on television, radio and in everyday conversations, even if these sentences contain grammatical errors, but we rarely write full sentences in our written communications. We now read and write messages in incomplete sentences using abbreviated words, little punctuation, a very limited vocabulary, and sometimes all in lower case.

While Americans still read books, newspapers, magazines and other printed media, the statistics are alarming:
- 33% of high school graduates never read another book the rest of their lives
- 42% of college graduates never read another book
- 80% of families did not buy or read a book last year
- 70% of adults have not been in a book store in five years
- 69% read newspapers in print, website or mobile app.

Language is a very important part of culture. Humans learn almost everything they know through language. Babies begin learning language the day they are born. Children acquire 80% of their total lifetime knowledge by the age of five through the spoken word, observation, experience and senses. It is an absolute necessity that our children hear language spoken to them in grammatically complete sentences if they are going to learn to speak and write English correctly, but if we speak to them the way we now communicate on our electronic devices, we are going to end up with illiterate children, not ready for school. It is extremely hard for children to learn how to speak and write correctly if they have already internalized incorrect ways of speaking and writing.

Languages have a structure just like mathematics, and if the structure isn't correctly written or spoken the result is incorrect, just like an incorrectly done math problem. If we are not reading books, and the statistics say that we aren't, then we are not only missing out

82

on how English is properly written, we are also failing to acquire a good vocabulary. The English language has a very rich and large vocabulary, but the size of the vocabulary used in our literature and spoken has decreased significantly in the last 50 years.

Recently, there has been much publicity about the widening financial gap between the middle and upper classes. This has come about because of the very different views the Right and Left have of how America's economy should function. The Right has convinced its base that the widening financial gap is a good thing and that the wealthy should not have to pay more taxes because they are the job creators.

The words "Read my lips, no new taxes" uttered by President George H. W. Bush during his Presidency (Jan. 20, 1989 to Jan. 20, 1993) became the Right's battle cry. The Right has convinced many American people that taxes, per se, are bad, and wealthier citizens of the United States should pay a lower progressive rate than they now do. While collecting less tax, Right-controlled state legislators cut the amount of tax money going toward public education to 'balance' budgets. Members of the Right hold the Governorship's of many more states than the Left. The Governors of these states have convinced their base that both taxes and education are bad, and therefore very little tax money should go to the public schools. Many states also give tax money vouchers to help parents send their children to private or religious schools. A few states also give tax money vouchers to parents who home school their children. These practices are getting the results desired by the Right. Many Americans now think both education and taxes are bad. In order to stay a viable country good tax supported public schools are a must.

Evangelical Christians operate many private schools in our country that teach the Right's political and philosophical views. Public tax money is going to such schools. Tax money should not go religious educational institutions. Changing the United States Constitution to create a Theocracy is one of the goals of the Right. Americans should not be financing the campaign to accomplish that goal.

America's school age youth are frightened. They live with the constant of threat of gun violence disrupting their lives. Our children fear for their lives every day at school, as well as when they attend movies, eat in a fast food restaurant, attend a concert, or just walk down the street. Parents now drive their children to and from school, and to places of entertainment, or even to a friend's house just around the corner. Gun violence in the United states is higher than any other country on Earth. The United States has 88.8 guns for every 100 residents. Our country's death rate by firearms is 10.2 per 10,000 people. The 2nd highest is Finland with 3.6 per 10,000 people. Japan and The Republic of Korea have zero. Our elected officials refuse to do anything about gun violence and won't even debate it although polling shows a majority of Americans desire some action. What one can conclude from the above is that our legislators are being bribed to turn away from the problem. With a population of over 300 million people living in the United States, there has been no mass movement to stop this horrible carnage. Recently, survivors of the Parkland, Florida's school shootings have decided to do something about stopping the gun atrocities going on in United States. Let us hope the adults can come to their senses and help them.

Children who don't feel safe, who are not allowed to travel on their own, and who are getting the wrong message about their accountability for school performance, grow up lacking self confidence, and are less eager to embrace adulthood. It is not unusual for today's teenagers to put off getting their drivers licenses until they are much older than the legal age to drive. Children more often live with their parents far into adulthood, and have a hard time taking on adult responsibilities. Depression and anxiety is a common characteristic of this group. Children understand that they don't have much to look forward to when they leave school. Their parents are working 10 hour days, or have two or more jobs, just to make ends meet. Even highly paid tech jobs require a lot of servitude, and often long hours. We Americans work longer hours, have fewer sick days, less vacation days and fewer benefits than any other highly civilized country in the world.

This is a radical change from my youth in the 40's and 50's. My dad was an engineer and my mother a teacher. My family took a vacation every year. I had visited all lower 48 states as well as Canada and Mexico by the time I was 17. My father was home for dinner at 6:00 every night, and didn't leave for work until 8:00 in the morning. He had every weekend off plus all national holidays. My dad was a highly regarded engineer who held two patents for innovations in his field. He loved to work in his workshop in the garage and did all of the handyman chores around the house. Yes, we were upper middle class, but all middle class people in those days who had a job had benefits similar to my dad, and only a single wage-earner supported a family. Other middle-classers possibly didn't do as much traveling or live in quite as nice a neighborhood, but they had vacations, 8-5 work hours and weekends and holidays off. Students completing school in those days believed they could accomplish great things if they applied themselves to the task. Americans felt they were living successful, happy and rewarding lives.

Today's workers don't live the same lifestyle or enjoy the same benefits and our children know it. Present day Americans do not feel they are living successful, happy and rewarding lives. Since the accepted definition for success has now become making lots of money, Americans have chosen to work like slave labor, devoting their entire lives to their jobs, hoping to to attain the trappings of the good life by working as many hours as possible, even at high paying jobs, in order to live in a nice home, and drive a nice car. Some just give up and consider themselves unsuccessful. Americans capitulation to the Right is making it easy for the Right to succeed in their mission of molding the United States government to their liking. Our nation's populous have been brain washed by the philosophy of a cabal who believe they are the most successful people in the world because of the amounts of money they have. The Right believes Americans should revere them and surrender their lives to them. By making money the only road to success, the Right has doomed the entire population of the United States to lives of servitude and unhappiness.

America's public schools have been responsible for the implementation of the Left's views as well which clash with the Right's in part, because they require large expenditures for people not in the upper class. Public schools have been the leaders in both the integration of blacks and immigrants into main stream society. America's teachers have done the job with a deep sense of responsibility and the desire to succeed. It took an enormous amount of effort and training to learn how to teach English Language Learners and to understand the cultures of each group of minorities and/or immigrants in order to teach those children how learn to succeed in their new environment.

Public schools have also been the leaders in the acceptance of children with special mental or physical needs. By law, every child including the disabled has a right to a public school education. Enormous amounts of money has been spent to make school buildings compliant for special needs children, and to train Special Education teachers in the specialty of teaching disabled children.

America's teachers have helped our nations' children learn to accept the current social mores, including less traditional family structures and tolerance of people of all cultures and lifestyles. Our teachers have done an amazing job of leading both children and adults in the acceptance of the enormous changes that have taken place in American society over the past 50 years, and 70% of Americans think these changes are good.

The Right has overblown the role immigrants and minorities have played in the decline of America's public schools. For reasons discussed in previous chapters, our student's standardized test scores have gone down. President George W. Bush's education bill, "No Child Left Behind," was based on test taking for all students including the disabled and those new to the system. Averages of all of the test scores were used to rate our schools. Schools with the highest number of minority and immigrant children did poorly. Students in the more affluent and less racially mixed areas are doing very well. Immigrant children aren't ruining the public school system, in fact as they go through the public school system they begin to catch up and do as well as the rest of the student population. The Right has used the low standardized test scores from certain areas to prove that blacks, immigrants, and people with alternative lifestyles are ruining our schools. The Right has used this information to turn the American people against public education. The Right has been successful. 30% percent of Americans believe that blacks, immigrants, and those with alternative lifestyles have ruined America, and that any successes they have achieved have been at the expense of whites. The Right has encouraged their base to use violence against these less worthy people to rid them from our midst. All that a lower overall test score proves is that the demographics have changed – the system has the same ability to educate as in the past. The system is not doing a poorer job.

How is it that the Right, with only 30% of Americans backing them, as compared to 70% of Americans that don't, succeed in taking over America's state and federal Governments? The answer is not complicated. Due to the great population shifts over the last 50 years, half of the people of the United States now live in just 9 states.

These states are:

- California
- Texas
- Illinois
- Michigan
- New York
- Ohio
- Pennsylvania
- Georgia
- Florida

The other half of the population is distributed among the remaining 41 states. Each of the 50 states have two Senators representing them in the Senate. Currently, half of the population of the United States is represented in Congress by only 18 Senators, and half by the remaining 82 Senators. This lopsided imbalance has favored the Right because the less populous states represented by the 82 tend to be rural and conservative. Twenty of the less populous states are solidly red, and seven more lean toward the Right. The Right spent many millions of dollars to insure enough of the less populous states would vote Right in the 2016 Presidential election to assure the Electoral College vote would favor Trump (and the minority view of Americans), and thus assure a Presidential win, even though The Left's candidate won the popular vote.

The outcome of the 2016 Presidential Election has proved to be devastating for teachers. The new President and his administration are more anti education than any previous administration. The Secretary of Education, Betsy De Vos, is anti public schools.... America's Secretary of Education is anti education!

The most significant consequence of our failing public school system is what it signifies about the state of our society. The rest of the world's leaders are working on alternative energy, water conservation, modern infrastructures, universal health care, and building strong economies, while in the United States a handful of very wealthy zealots are rapidly changing the United States of America into a failing third world country.

Solutions

There is no single 'magic bullet' to make the public school system 'Great Again.' There are obvious changes that should be made to readjust the way the system is funded and controlled to adjust it to a new reality in our society.

Providing adequate financing for our public schools, and paying our teachers adequately would help restore America's public schools to the position in our society necessary for our country's prosperity, and well being. We must provide these funds though a fair, equitable and adequate tax policy.

Taxes are necessary to pay our nation's expenses. How much taxes are collected and what government expenses are covered is part of all state and federal constitutions. Article I, Section 8 of the Constitution of the United States states:

> "The Congress shall have Power to Lay and collect taxes, Duties, Imports and Excises, to pay debts and provide for the common Defense and General Welfare of the United States; but all Duties, Imports and Excises shall be uniform throughout the United States;"

A successful society's tax code must provide for all governmental needs. More money is required to finance a growing and prosperous society than a decaying society. Today's prosperous societies provide for the poor, health care for all, the construction and upkeep of the infrastructure, an education system, a defense system and more.

> The opening paragraph of the Constitution states that the People should "promote the common Welfare."

The Right and Left interpret the meaning of "common welfare" very differently as well as the means to promote it. Financial provision for promoting welfare is made through the collection of taxes. To the Right, fairness in tax collection means that we all pay tax, equal on a per-person basis; if some of us have become more successful (wealthier) we should be able to keep our wealth. If there was more equality in wages, The Rights' view would carry some weight. This is unrealistic in a capitalistic democracy. On the other hand, The Left views taxes as part of the social means to equalize wages and welfare. They believe in taxation that rises proportionally with the ability (true ability in terms of net financial worth without loopholes) to pay. Due to current law permitting legislators to receive virtually unlimited campaign funds from anonymous sources under the guise of 'free speech', neither Right nor Left approaches are likely to be adopted in pure form. Continued compromises only muddy the tax codes further.

The current US tax code doesn't provide adequate funds for all government operations or public services. Money speaks loudly to our politicians; the wealthiest individuals and industries get the politicians' ears while many worthy causes are not heard. Currently, America's tax policies place the largest tax burden on those with the least ability to pay. Those most able to pay, pay very little in percentage of earnings or net worth. This is not fair, equitable, nor does it provide an adequate amount of revenue to pay America's bills. If wage earners don't make enough money to pay their own bills, how can they be expected to also pay their country's bills? Government programs that assist the poor or provide social services to other than the rich are being cut or eliminated to fund the military. The Affordable Care Act, Medicaid and Medicare have either been slashed or are on the chopping block. Our public schools are among the biggest losers.

The wealthy leadership of the Right is putting our entire country at risk of financial ruin. Our whole economic system will collapse if new tax policies aren't put in place that tax the wealthy for their fair share. Working Americans, who make a fraction of the income of CEO's can't sustain the United States government by themselves. The wealthy will have to return some of working America's money by paying their fair share of taxes. "No new taxes" can never be the policy of a highly civilized society. Americans have tried that policy for years, and it has failed. The over 300 million American majority must stand up for our country and change the tax laws for the benefit of everyone.

Americans spend over 50% of the federal budget on the military. We spend more on our military than any other country in the world. The US spent $618 billion on its military last year, more than 3 times the 171 billion budget of 2nd place China. This should put us far above other nations in military power. Yet, we are told we need to spend even more money to build a more competitive military. How can this be if we spend so much more money than every other country? Something is wrong, and the public needs to understand what that is. If our military budget was cut by a modest amount, it is unlikely we would lose our competitiveness and we could spend the rest of the money to finance our failing infrastructure and public schools.

Americans must elect candidates to both state and federal legislative bodies who are both pro-education and for a fair and equitable tax code. Current legislators from the Left have attempted to get pro-education and fair tax laws passed, but they have been continually blocked by Right. Americans must elect Democrats or those who lean Left in order to change the current unfair and destructive policies. Older Americans associate Republicans with an upper middle class that stood for monetary success, strong morals, traditional Christian values, traditional families and social mores, but those are just fond memories. Republicans no longer adhere to platforms of the past; they have been hijacked by the Right (refer to Chapter III for current platforms).

Americans must study legislative candidates' agendas and their voting records carefully and thoroughly. It is not enough to just listen to what a candidate says in speeches, advertisements, or endorsements by celebrities or friends. Candidates often gear their speeches and ads to a particular audience, play to peoples emotions, or lie. The best way to know a candidate is to study their voting records in order to understand the policies they actually support. Very often a legislator will tell the public one thing and then soon after, vote the opposite. If the candidate has never held office, then voting on the basis of their party affiliation is probably best.

The key to getting candidates you want to win is to vote. Voting is the only way of having your voice heard. Yes, your vote does count. Very often, only a few votes will decide an outcome one way or the other. Americans have a very poor voting record. A 60% voting turnout is very high and happens only during Presidential Election years. If the American public desires change, then they must vote for it. Not voting assures the continuing decline of our great nation.

Properly funding America's schools and paying teachers in line with other professionals would be a big step toward saving our public schools, but if teachers are to improve their lot, they will have to stand up for themselves. To be considered professionals teachers will have to demand the respect and compensation accorded professionals. We have seen that good teachers are leaving the field in great numbers, fed up with poor working conditions, low pay and lack of respect within and outside of education. No one but the teachers, themselves, can do much about the situation. It is time to put the collective teacher's foot down. Enough is enough! Teacher organizations must spend time and money on public relations. They must quit being defensive and move on the offensive to counter the negative publicity with more positive campaigns in support of their profession. Teachers need to make more of an effort to toot their own horns.

When our schools began to notice the change in students due to changes in the home and in society, an effort was begun to enlist parent interest and help for their children and schools. In order to accomplish this goal, parents were asked to help in the classroom, form fund raising and parent support groups, join text book selection committees, curriculum committees and the like. On the surface all this seemed progressive and a good idea to pique parents' interest in schools. In actuality, it created a monster that began to attack teachers! Any human who is asked for advice will try very hard to do just that whether they know anything about the subject or not. It is also human nature to elevate the advice giver above the advice seeker. Therefore, parents, and especially those in school 'support' groups, became experts in the education and purported to know far more than teachers and even school boards and administrators. These parent groups watch teachers like hawks and are overly critical; their critiques had little to do with the true effectiveness of a teacher or school. An even bigger shame is that administrators are very threatened by these parents, leaving the teachers without any kind of positive reinforcement or support.

Parents and other members of the general public have come to have too much authority in the schools. Major policies, financial, curriculum, physical plant use and more are greatly influenced, if not actually made, by lay people other than teachers and administrators. Teachers need to take control of their own profession. Teachers, front-line experts in education through training and experience, should have a significant part in decisions concerning curriculum, teaching methods, discipline and other factors concerned with the actual classroom.

One argument that always arises when talking about the problem of control is that because schools are tax supported, the public has the right to run the schools as they choose, not just financially, but with methodology of teaching content, in discipline, and parent involvement. While ultimately true, the public decides how public education is to be conducted through the legislative process. While public input is necessary, ultimately the law and those policies and procedures derived from the law determine how the schools are run. Local control must only flesh out the details that has (hopefully) been determined by educational professionals in concert with legislators. State and federal law determine rules on (for example) age limits, the eligibility of the sexes, and citizenship requirements.

Let's draw an analogy to make this point a bit more clear. Let's say that the public votes to build a new roadway to alleviate a traffic problem. Once the decision is made through public hearings that a roadway should be built, engineers, construction workers and others trained to design and build roadways take over and do the job. The public has no say as to how the actual pavement is put down – even though roadway construction is paid for with tax money. Schools should be run the same way.

Teachers should not allow laymen to continue making decisions concerning teacher training, teacher evaluations, teacher job descriptions and the like. This should be left up to the educators; those trained and experienced in public school education.

I have always dreamed of planning the curriculum for my classes exactly the way I think it should be. I'm sure other teachers feel the same way. Over the past few decades the curriculum for our schools has been cut to the bone. Music, Art, Drama, Library and even P. E. have been eliminated from many elementary schools and even middle schools. One school where I taught emphasized a curriculum in reading, writing and math with science and social studies taught on alternate days. The rationale was that English Language Learners, the disabled, less able learners, and the like would benefit from extra-concentrated lessons plus an extended class time of 90 minutes for learning reading, language arts, and math. This decision, which was made by non-teachers, is very unsound. The average student has an approximate 20 to 30 minute time limit for learning new material. It doesn't matter what a teacher does; after 20 to 30 minutes on a particular subject, learning time is over….period. Any class on an extended time schedule of 90 minutes leaves 70 minutes of every period for the teacher to try everything in his/her power to do the impossible. Students become just as bored, frustrated, and tired as the teachers and no learning takes place under these circumstances. Traditionally class time was divided into 50 to 55 minute periods. That gave the teacher enough time to take the roll 5 min., review the previous lesson 10 min., present new material 20 min. then a reinforcement activity for the new material 20 min. This is a proven formula for optimum learning. Ninety minute periods waste 30 minutes of time and both students and teachers.

Spare time is not a waste of time. Everyone needs time to relax, be alone, think and get to know themselves. Students need spare time to digest what they are being taught. What we learn is stored in our subconscious, and becomes available to our conscious brain when needed. The more we actually learn and store away, the more knowledge we have to call upon when information is needed. Our brains can't store information if we don't give it enough time to do so. College classes are given three times a week for a reason. The time in between classes gives the brain the time it needs to process the new information. Younger students need spare time, too. Keeping them busy with all kinds of activities is not necessarily good. Children need spare time in order to process what they are being taught. Schools should have more breaks, play times, and quiet times to allow for maximum learning.

Physical Education, art, music, health and social skills, are all important to the development of well rounded, responsible and happy individuals. The variety and fun in these activities make children want to come to school. Within these activities, the academic curriculum is also advanced through language, measurement, etc. It has been proven that children exposed to music learn more and at a faster rate than children who aren't, yet we continue to cut music from our public school curriculum. In fact, we have cut almost every subject that is fun, interesting and facilitates learning. A child will learn to read and understand the meaning of words in a song very quickly and will expand their vocabularies in science, music, PE and art classes. Any subject that is interesting and fun teaches reading, language arts and even math comprehension, and expands skills learned in academic classes. Children need to do things themselves, and learn about themselves.

The perfect curriculum for all children from pre-school through 12th grade would include the following:

- Reading and Language Arts
- Mathematics
- Social Studies, including history, geography, archaeology, civics, climate, economics
- Science, including physics, chemistry, astronomy, biology, astronomy, botany, zoology, geology, Earth Science, health
- Electronic media skills
- Physical Education
- Art, including art appreciation, painting, drawing, sculpture, crafts, color, mediums
- Music, including voice, band, orchestra, music appreciation
- Family living skills, including finances, nutrition, personal relationships, household management, household repairs and more

Parents must become more supportive of the teachers and better disciplinarians of their own children. It isn't the teachers who need to be disciplined; it is the students. Parents need to understand that their children misbehave in school, either blatantly, or through subterfuge because of the attitudes they have learned either at home or at other activities outside of school experiences. Parents do not help their children by supporting groups that belittle teachers and give the message that parents know more than the teachers. Support for the schools should come from being better parents. Students who are loved, well trained, well fed, disciplined and cared for at home, do well in school. Let's permit the teachers be the experts at schooling.

Throughout the history of the United States of America, The Declaration of Independence has been quoted over and over again to prove that all people are created equal. But what does being "equal" mean? The authors of the Declaration, and its signers, did not believe all people are created equal. At the time the Declaration was written, the authors and signers were only talking about white male landowners. Slaves, indentured servants, women and non land owners were not considered equal. Even white men were only considered equal in that their life should not be taken, that they should have freedom from arbitrary or despotic government control and should be able to do things that would bring them happiness. The Declaration was not intended to express that all humans were equal in any other way. Today, most students are taught that all men and women are equal in the eyes of the law and have equal opportunity.

"All men are created equal" has been interpreted and distorted by the public to mean that every child should receive identical opportunity for instruction, regardless of learning ability or interest. Many of our public school policies have been developed to implement teaching methodologies utilizing this concept. Experienced teachers understand that each and every child is precious, and should be treated with respect and care, but they also know that each child has different abilities and talents. For too long, our schools have been laboring to bring the poorer students up to the level of the better performing students. We are spending far too much of our educational resources, in time, materials and personnel, trying to teach those who are unable or unprepared to learn. We are doing this at the great expense of our brightest and best teachers and students. While placing our emphasis on bringing the poor students up a point or two on a test, we are dragging our greatest resource - the brightest and best students - down into a sea of mediocrity and waste. Society cannot blame teachers for this enormous debacle; it is virtually impossible to provide the same high-level result using a common curriculum, taught in a common time-scale to class that has widely varying capability and readiness to learn. Teachers and students alike recognize the futility of this approach. If we are going to improve the educational needs of America's children, we must put aside the notion that all children can become educated, and allow those who are capable and who want to learn move forward. This is not to say that each child does not deserve the same opportunity to learn, but it is up to the individual student to put forth the effort and thus obtain from their education what he/she is willing to put into it. We also have to realize that a range of outcomes are equally valid; there is no difference in worth among those who become craftsmen, artists, soldiers, or professors.

I am reminded of a story about my youngest daughter. At the age of six she joined the swim team at our local pool. She was one of about thirty in the 'six and under' group. Only four swimmers from this group could swim in the scoring heats of each meet. The others swam in non-scoring heats. The winners of the first heats received the traditional blue, red or white place ribbons while the other participants received an orange participation ribbon. In the first meet in which my daughter swam, she did not get anything but orange ribbons. I made a big fuss over them and tried to camouflage the fact that they had no meaning. As I was gushing on about how proud I was, my six year old calmly explained that these were only participation ribbons and that she had not been in any race that counted. She accepted this with grace and pride. I was the only one that had a problem.

I've related this anecdote to illustrate the point that children know their own strengths and weaknesses and can accept both. Children are also quite capable of understanding their peers and placing them in proper perspective. Administrative policies should not be based on the assumption that all children are equal and that those children would be upset if some got better grades or were recognized otherwise for achievement. It is a 'life-lesson' to not always 'win' and sometimes to be embarrassed or upset if they don't receive the same acclaim as their peers.

In order to improve our educational standards, grouping children by ability is essential. It is just as much of a disservice to a child to place him/her in a class above his/her ability level as it is to put a bright child in with others who are below his/her ability level. It is far easier for teachers to teach classes of like ability than to teach classes of students of mixed ability.

This can be likened to a classical medical triage. In a mass casualty event, a room full of injured are either terminal, moderately injured, but curable, and the remainder are only mildly injured and don't need immediate attention. Lay people ask the doctor to give his attention to all of the patients although he is fully aware that some cannot recover. He is trained to help only those who have a chance of survival and only keep the others comfortable. But a lay person who has no intimate knowledge of the patients' conditions will typically demand that the doctor concentrate all of his efforts on those who are least likely to recover; this situation will result in more patients dying. This, in essence, is what our educational policies are doing to our children. We cannot concentrate on the weak and expect the strong to survive.

Mainstreaming 'special needs' children into regular classrooms causes enormous problems for the regular classroom teacher. The reasoning behind this movement is that the special needs child would benefit from being in a class with regular students by feeling more included in the school and school activities, thus achieving more academically and socially. While this might be true, it comes at great expense for the other students and the regular classroom teacher. Learning is compromised for the regular students and it is just one more job for the regular classroom teacher.

The above is is an example of rule-by-exception. Rule-by-exception is now common in our public schools. Often, a student will not be punished for a misdeed for which others have received punishment, or not be required to do an assignment for a reason that other students aren't entitled to use. Parent request, social standing, favoritism and the like are used as excuses for this type of behavior. Examples of this are rampant in communities where certain school sports are a major part of community events. This isn't fair to the rest of the students, and it takes respect and credibility away from teachers.

People choose communities in which to live according to family income, geographical location, climate, jobs, family, race, religion, hobbies, availability of sporting opportunities, schools and more. Income is a large factor when choosing a home. It is human nature to want to live in a place where one feels safe, comfortable, prideful, happy and more. One way to improve educational opportunities for our children is to re-establish community schools. Neighborhoods are most often identified by race and level of income. We need as a society to stop fighting human nature and instead make schools more representative of the communities in which they are established.

It takes time to adjust to change. Over time most people adjust to the changes in their lives, but in today's society, change is rampant in every sector, and happening at a rapid rate. Most people haven't had time to adjust. Perhaps we need to stop pushing so hard on so many social issues. I don't mean that we should abandon the progress we have made. Just allow the public a little slack and let nature take its course.

Violence caused by racism, same sex marriage, gay rights, transgender rights, and immigration is a direct result of our population being pushed faster than they can adjust to the new norms. Whites feel especially threatened as they are becoming fewer in number while other racial groups become larger. Media coverage of these events makes it appear as if there are vast numbers of people in all of these groups and that they are taking over our entire nation. This is not true, but people, especially whites, are acting as if it is true.

According to the 2010 census we are:
- 63.7 % White
- 16.3 % Hispanic or Latino
- 12.2 % Black
- 4.7 % Asian
- 1.9 % Mixed Race
- 10 % All others

3.8 % of our population is Gay or Lesbian

Humans prefer to associate with those having a similar background. It is human nature to do so. I had a neighbor who was the childrens' librarian at our city library. We often talked about the problems both our schools and the population in general was having because of the rapid growth of racial diversity in our community.

During one of these discussions my neighbor told this story: Students from the nearby high school came to the library after school to do their home work. So many were using the facility they expanded the children's section to better accommodate this group. Part of the plan was to add tables to encourage interracial seating. No matter what methods they tried to achieve interracial seating it didn't work. Asian students sat at one table, the Hispanics at another table, the Whites at another table and so on.

Returning to the community school concept is advantageous in other ways: Instead of transporting students long distances to go to a school that meets narrow academic or social needs, we should instead make every school in every neighborhood offer the same educational opportunities of a rigorous and complete curriculum as every other school. Children would feel more comfortable in a familiar environment, spend less travel time, and the school would likely be a more popular gathering place for both educational and social events. In some communities, additional specialized schools for the arts or science supplement community schools where the demand in smaller individual schools would not be great enough to warrant advanced specialized curriculum; this has been done successfully for many years in places such as New York City.

Recently, the parents of a public school student won a lawsuit in which they claimed the local school district should pay for a particular student's education in a special private school located in another state because the local system had failed to diagnose a special learning disability, and therefore this child had not gotten a proper education. This case points to the enormous misconception of the purpose of public education. First, the verdict implies the release of parents from any educational responsibility for their child, placing it all on the school. Secondly, it sets a precedent that could be the death knell of public schools. This might sound a little extreme, but just think about it: Can we sue our local school system because we feel the local system is not providing special facilities or very high level tutelage for our gifted child? Can we demand a special school for him/her? How specialized must public education become to deal with a small minority of children who might be helped by special private schools? If the reaction to this decision is to remove limits to what schools must provide, schools are in big trouble. The school system should never have given in to those parents. What ever happened to parent responsibility? No educational progress can be made until parents of this nation regain control and take responsibility for their offspring. Teachers cannot and should not be both parents and teacher to their students.

Better pay, better working conditions, more responsible parents, student ability groupings, better (and more complete) curriculum, plus a basic change in attitude will help teachers. If we as a nation are not willing to do something for teachers, we are not going to have any teachers nor will we have our public schools. The public, as well as administrators and politicians, do not believe this can happen. They think that if every public school teacher walked off the job, there would be others anxiously waiting to take their place, and worse, many of our teachers believe the same to be true. It is not true. There are thousand of teaching positions going unfilled all across our country; in Arizona alone, there are 2,000 unfilled positions. Certified teachers who are not working in the field have gone on to higher paying or more rewarding jobs. Any prior excess is gone, and our system as we know it, will also be gone if we don't do something about it.

Because of the social and political weakness of the teachers, top level politicians, especially governors, have been able to strengthen their own political positions by denigrating teachers. It is as possible to find incompetent teachers as one can find incompetents in any group and in any profession. One could even be so bold as to say some of our politicians are less than perfect! However, political leaders routinely target teachers for their own political gain, and this abuse must be brought to a halt. We cannot continue to put all the blame for lower test scores, or for poorly equipped graduates on our teachers. Furthermore, we cannot ignore the fact that our schools, despite all the social upheaval, phenomenal technical progress and legislative changes in the last 50 years, have turned out quantities of well educated, fully equipped students ready to take on today's problems. No, teachers are not stupid, just as our students do not all have behavior problems or are unequipped to learn. Let us, instead of attacking teachers, attack the real problems in education and save our schools.

Food for Thought

History tells us to beware of some fundamental factors that portend the deterioration of a society. Public Education can be a bulwark against the fall of our most cherished rights and institutions.

This chapter begins with a history lesson. At the end of the lesson it will be clear as to what more we can do to stop the tragic and rapid failure of our educational system. This will ensure that we, as a society, won't drift backwards, but keep going forward with the reforms we need to make the United Sates current with other advanced countries in the World.

I taught Social Studies at the Jr. High and Middle School levels for many years. Teaching history was extremely rewarding to me. I especially enjoyed teaching sixth grade Social Studies. The curriculum covered the development of Human Civilizations from before written history to the fall of the Roman Empire. The lessons integrated other Social Studies subjects such as Geography, Weather and Climate, Government, Economics and Archaeology into the curriculum, making human history so much more understandable and fun. These lessons are important to review, or to learn for the first time, as we must understand the past in order to make good decisions about the present and the future.

Here are some of the salient points I made while teaching 6th grade Social Studies:
- Today's' humans are basically the same both physically and mentally as humans were thousands of years ago.
- Geography and climate have had an enormous influence in the shaping of human history.
- Civilizations have a life span, are established and disappear like everything else.
- Throughout the world, all humans have the same basic needs.

These are the five basic needs listed in order of survival time if they are denied, from shortest to longest:

- Air
- Water
- Food
- Clothing
- Shelter

I have added a 6th that after teaching for so many years, I have found to be just as vital to life as the others:

- Love and care.

There is not a human on Earth who can survive without these six needs being met.

Humans have provided their basic needs by living in cooperative groups such as extended families, tribes, or more complex groups called societies, cultures, or civilizations. These groups formed to more efficiently provide the basic need and wants of human populations that individuals cannot supply for themselves. Here is a list of components that comprise a civilization:

- A stable supply of fresh water - (This is a recent addition because water is no longer a given, as it was in the past.)
- A stable and adequate food supply
- A diversity of labor
- An effective government
- A culture
- A class system

If one of these components of a civilization fails, the entire civilization is at risk of failure. Civilizations can not survive without the functioning of each of these six components. Collapse of a civilization can happen through gradual change until all the components are substantially different, or through a complete and rapid breakdown of several of the components.

Civilizations are often referred to as Societies or Cultures. These labels can be used interchangeably, but Societies are defined as smaller sub-groups of a larger civilization. The United States is basically a part of the Civilization of the Western World.

How is the United States fairing as a society? Let's examine the current and past states of each of the components:

A stable supply of clean water
The United States has a vast supply of both fresh and salt water. We have the Atlantic Ocean along the East Coast, the Gulf of Mexico, and the Pacific Ocean along our West Coast. The Mississippi River System is the third largest in the world. The Colorado River runs from Colorado all the way to Mexico. The Columbia serves the Northwest. The Great lakes have 84% of North America's fresh water. Large underground aquifers provide water for our vast plains and deserts. We should have enough fresh water for all of our basic needs. But that is not the case at present.

Since the beginning of the Industrial Revolution of the late 1800's and early 1900's our rivers, lakes and oceans have become increasingly polluted. Toxins, human, animal, and agricultural waste were dumped into our most valuable water sources before these practices were regulated. Government regulations to halt the pollution of our waters were passed and implemented, but more recently the Right has been successful in dismantling our regulatory system, and once again our water sources are being contaminated by all types of industrial, agricultural and human waste.

An example of a regulatory problem are the underground pipelines transporting oil under our farmlands and cities. They are constantly breaking, causing property damage, and polluting both water and soil. Foreign oil companies are building an oil pipeline from Canada to port cities located along the Gulf of Mexico, with the oil flowing through these pipes being shipped to other countries. The pipelines are putting our aquifers in danger. We were told that the pipe lines would bring thousands of jobs to Americans, but very few permanent oil pipeline jobs were created. It appears that the Right put wealth and power far above the needs of America and our citizens' basic needs.

The Right is very good at diverting Society's attention away from or lying about what is really happening to our country's water supply. Native Americans put up a big fight over the building of the Canadian pipeline that they feared would put their water supply in danger of contamination. They had the backing of many other Americans, but in the end, state and federal troops were sent in to halt the protests, and the Native Americans had to give up. These Americans were threatened, violated, demonized and used as an example of how bad people were getting in the way of good, patriotic, law abiding citizens. In fact, it was the opposite. Americans will not receive any substantial benefit from the pipelines, while their existence puts our water supplies in danger. Unfortunately, the majority of the American people agreed with the Right's argument. The public let their prejudices get in the way of the facts.

We are being taken in by a group using our land and water supply for their own gain, destroying it in the process, and our government is allowing this to happen. Our water is being polluted by industrial waste from industries that use our natural resources to make a very few people rich, and the results can be seen everywhere in the United States. An important example is the effect of fracking on local well water. State governments were enticed by job creation and tax revenue offered by permitting widespread fracking. Companies claimed that technology would prevent contamination of ground water. However, many water wells in the rural areas around the fracking sites began to show substantial amounts of pollutants, some carcinogenic. The solution offered was to provide bottled water for drinking. This is an abuse of homeowners as they have no other recourse, their property values have decreased, and they will suffer inconvenience (or worse) in perpetuity.

Flint, Michigan's water is no longer usable for drinking, or much of anything else. This is due to failure to maintain infrastructure to current standards, compounded by lack of means to finance it plus government denial that there was even a problem. Imagine how it would be to not be able to get fresh water out of your home's faucets. How would you cook, shower, and clean? Flushing the toilet would be about the only use of your house water. Drinking water has to come from bottled water. Flint is an American city without fresh water. What city will be next?

Pollution isn't the only reason our supply of fresh water is dwindling. In some areas of the country we are running out of water because of overpopulation and/or drought. Large cities in the southwest such as Phoenix, Las Vegas, Tucson, and their suburbs, as well as southern California's Imperial Valley, a large agricultural area, are running out of water. The Colorado River is the main source of water for that vast area. The Salt River used to be the primary source of water for the Phoenix area, but no longer meets the needs of the city or its fast growing suburbs. One can just imagine what would happen if these cities should run out of water. Arizona's economy is driven by ever-expanding housing with little attention to the overall water problem.

The south and east coasts of the United States are facing other water problems, mainly one of too much water. More rain than usual is causing major flooding in these regions and rising ocean levels are causing problems along the east coast. Hurricanes are increasing in quantity and intensity; the denuding of coastal areas to benefit the petroleum industry have resulted in increased damage to places like New Orleans. Puerto Rico has suffered from hurricanes' increased intensity. Government help has been slow and has accomplished little towards helping these areas recover. Flood waters are dirty and contain toxins and human waste and as such contaminate the fresh water supply. Our nation's fresh water supply, especially in these areas, is in danger, and showing signs of great stress.

A stable and adequate food supply

The land within the borders of the United State of America is prime real estate. We are third in the world in land suitable for agriculture. Our nation's farmers grow enough food for everyone in our own country and export vast amounts as well. Then why do millions of America's children and adults go to bed hungry every night? One reason may be that many Americans don't consider the underfed to be Americans because they are immigrants or minorities, so it doesn't matter. Possibly, they don't know that more white children go to bed hungry than the other two groups combined, or maybe they just don't care about poor white people either.

It is not a shortage of food that is causing so many of Americas' people to go hungry. Attitudes of the American people and Government policies are responsible, but the way food is distributed is also responsible. Large corporations, with very few regulations, have been allowed by our Federal Government to control to a great degree what our farmers grow, how the crops are processed, marketed and sold. Crops, cattle, hogs, eggs, just about every type of food raised or grown on our land, goes to large corporate owned possessing plants. These corporations maintain a monopoly on food supply. They can process and distribute the kinds of products they wish to make, charge any price they wish to charge, and sell the products in any market they choose, foreign or domestic. Government regulates trade, but most trade agreements favor the corporations. Even if a tariff is placed on an American farmers' crop, and other countries start buying that crop from another country, the farmers of that particular crop get hurt, but it doesn't change in any way how food is distributed in the United States. There is basically no other way to obtain food in America than to buy it at the supermarket, restaurants, or big box stores. Yes, we do have backyard gardens, co-ops that grow food on empty lots, and Farmers' Markets supplied by farms that are too small for corporate buyers, but these growers don't put much of a dent in the food needs of the American people.

With this type of food distribution system, the only way to obtain food is to have enough money to purchase it. Since millions of Americans are living in poverty, or close to it, many families and individuals can't afford food, and the Government isn't much help; therefore, they and their children go to bed hungry night after night.

The way we distribute our food is also a cause for concern. Very little food is produced near the place it is consumed. Trucks, trains, airplanes and ships transport our food to every corner of our nation. The transporting of our food could be interrupted several ways: Fuel shortages, natural disasters, failing roads and bridges or massive storms can delay or even destroy food shipments. We've seen how quickly supermarket shelves empty during disruptions of any kind. Although the entire nation is not likely to be affected in a major way by a breakdown in the food distribution system in one area, any break in the system can impact the remainder, just like airline flight cancellations at one airport cause problems at other airports, often hundreds of miles away.

The destruction of our water supplies and land is causing farmers to greatly change the way they farm. Over-use of the aquifers during the 50's through the 70's depleted the water level so much that farmers have had to change crops grown and the way they irrigate them to use much less water. Climate change is having its effect on our agricultural production. Floods have wiped out crops, and changing temperatures are causing farmers to plant some crops earlier or later than in the very recent past, and in some areas, to plant only one crop each year instead of two.

Recently, government immigration policies have caused a lack of laborers to pick crops, so unpicked crops are being left to drop and rot on the ground. This hurts the income of the farmers, causes the price of these crops to rise, resulting in shortages at the supermarket.

Fracking in the Midwest, especially in Oklahoma, is causing earthquakes that cause damage to the land and buildings. This is a new and unnerving phenomenon in that part of the country.

A diversity of labor
Diversity of labor simply means that there are many types of jobs and occupations available. Globalization has lowered the diversity of labor-intensive jobs performed in America. Low cost transport permits us to design manufactured items here but have them assembled in lower labor cost countries. Gone are many the semi-skilled jobs such as bolting wheels and fenders on new cars; a higher level of education is required for newer jobs performed using automation. We are becoming a nation of banks, insurance companies, and warehouses. Our large medical industry must continue to exist within our borders, but it too is in turmoil because of inconsistent governmental policies and corporate greed.

An effective government
The United States of America is a Constitutional Democratic Republic. The federal government is made up of three distinct and equal branches: legislative, executive, and judicial. The legislative branch consists of the Senate and the House of Representatives that together are called Congress. The executive branch consists of the President, Vice President, and the Cabinet. The judicial branch consists of the Supreme Court and the lower courts. All of the powers of each branch are spelled out in the Constitution, but basically the legislature/Congress creates the laws, the executive enforces the laws and the judicial decides if the laws are constitutional. The Constitution has also been Amended in several significant ways reflecting the state of demographics, mores, and other factors at the time the Amendments were passed (Amendments require a significant amount of time to be passed plus assent by voters). The three branches of our government have equal powers, known as a system of checks and balances. The 50 states that comprise the United States of America, have their own constitutions, reflecting local concerns. State constitutions are

subordinate to the national constitution. Both the federal and state constitutions are the basis of law for each of their jurisdictions.

Recently, policies enacted by the elected officials of both the federal and state governments are stretching constitutional law close to the breaking point, and the tone and demeanor of these administrations is like no other administrations in the past. Their closeness to monies interests, hate, fear mongering and just general ineptness is doing great damage to our governments and our people. Our reputation in the rest of the world has plummeted.

One area in which our government is failing the public badly is gun control. How can our elected officials let the mass slaughter by gunfire continue? Legislators' lack of action to control guns in our country is unconscionable, and all citizens with any conscience, moral values, or religious beliefs should be calling their legislators on a daily basis, demanding that something be done. Why are students and teachers giving up their lives so that the Right can continue to endorse violent means?

Universal Medical Care, Medicaid for all, or any other type of government-paid medical insurance for the total population does not have wide-spread support. The Right is against all government sponsored programs, the majority of people are uncertain, and only a few who believe it is a good idea. This is because the Right has been putting out anti-universal health insurance coverage propaganda for well over 50 years. The rest of Western Civilization plus and many countries outside of our culture, have Universal Medical Coverage, and they are very satisfied with the state of medicine.

A culture
Our culture is basically our way of life. It consists of our language, religion, moral values, customs, traditions, the arts, and other characteristics of a population learned from birth, at home, school, and other outside environments. Culture constantly changes as technology increases, and as new people become a part of our society,

adding their food and other components of their culture to ours, enriching both. We, in the united States, have a rich and varied culture due to the many varied cultures brought to our shores by the earliest to the newest arrivals. We are a salad bowl of many and varied cultures from around the world.

Many Americans have had trouble accepting a multi-cultural society. While every new surge of immigrants to our shores has wakened anti-immigrant sentiment, our memories are short regarding how each has been assimilated and added to our culture. Recently, our differences, especially in religion and language, have activated White Supremacists, and their hatred of people of color and for those who speak a language other than English. The Right has also made cultural issues, such as abortion, primary political issues; no one is being forced to have an abortion. The government has gotten involved in many social issues or cultural concerns such as affirmative action, marriage and gender issues, taking the American people's attention away from government issues that should be of upmost importance. We are no longer a world leader because of this phenomenon.

A danger looming is that the Right wants to remove religion as a cultural component of our society and make it a governmental component. The Right wants Evangelical Christianity to be the official religion of the United States of America. This would not only be catastrophic, but unconstitutional as well. The first European settlers in America came here to escape religious persecution. As the colonies grew, people of other religious came from England, Germany, France, Holland, Spain and several other European countries, all seeking religious freedom. Our Founding Fathers (many, agnostic Masons) wrote in the Constitution that "Congress shall make no law respecting an establishment of religion, or prohibiting the free exercise thereof:". Making a specific religion part of our government would change our existing government and culture so much that it would cease to be the constitutional government we now have. The United States of America would no longer exist.

A class system
The class system is is the only component of our existing society that has already completely collapsed. Class systems, too, are always evolving, but ours has become so altered, and the change has happened so rapidly, that the prevalent the class system of the prior generation no longer exists.

A class system is necessary in a society because it defines everyone's place within the society and helps to maintain order. Without a class system, people feel uncomfortable and unsure of their relationships with others. Without well-defined class, it is hard to understand what you are supposed to do in many situations and what is expected of you. Class systems have a structure with specifications of where you, as an individual, belong. At present, the only defining fact that places an individual on any scale that measures significance in our society is the amount of money one has. Other considerations that define a person, such as character, background, values, education, occupation, talent, accomplishments or possessions have become minimized.

Older citizens feel especially disowned because the major characteristics of the class system they knew and worked so hard to achieve no longer exists. Older professionals used to be in the upper or upper middle class and were respected in their communities, but are now nowhere near the top of the pile. Corporate billionaires, sports stars and entertainers, with lots of money are the people on top now, and the rest of us have no means to ever advance to such an economic level.

The truncation and collapse of the class system is prevalent in all first-world nations. Globalization means that the ultra-rich can live anywhere and collect more wealth wherever it is advantageous at the moment. With the increase of world wide communication, travel, business, media coverage, social interactions, war, and more, the world's billionaires are at the top and everyone else below.

A tally of how the United States is fairing as a society measured by how well it is providing its people with the basic human needs, and how the components of our society are, or aren't functioning is as follows:

- Our class system is in complete failure.
- A fresh water supply, a stable food supply, a government and culture are in partial failure.
- Diversity of labor is decreasing

The future of the United States doesn't look good. Our society is not fully meeting the basic needs of our people. What can we do to meet the need now that we know we are failing? We need to restore, repair and re-create an educational system that will truly educate all of the members of our society in the basics, including an appreciation of the function of government. Only an educated populace can make good decisions to maintain a strong, healthy and functional society. If we want a country that provides its people with their basic needs plus so much more, then we have to make good schools our number one priority. The Right knows this which is why they are making the destruction of our public schools their number one priority. Educated people tend to be happier, healthier, more productive and make better decisions than the uneducated.

The Right has done everything they can to undermine our public schools, from preschool through university. In order to stop the damage already done by this very conservative UN-American group, we must take charge of our government by voting out those who wish to harm America and Americans, then vote in those who will once again make each of the components of our great society functional.

95169040R00066

Made in the USA
Lexington, KY
08 August 2018